THE SIMPLE LIFE

THE SIMPLE LIFE

HOW I FOUND HOME

Sarah Beeny

SEVEN DIALS

First published in Great Britain in 2023 by Seven Dials,
an imprint of The Orion Publishing Group Ltd
Carmelite House, 50 Victoria Embankment
London EC4Y 0DZ

An Hachette UK Company

3 5 7 9 10 8 6 4 2

A CIP catalogue record for this book is
available from the British Library.

All internal images courtesy of the author's personal collection.

ISBN (Hardback) 978 1 3996 1332 3
ISBN (Export Trade Paperback) 978 1 3996 1333 0
ISBN (eBook) 978 1 3996 1335 4
ISBN (Audio) 978 1 3996 1336 1

Typeset by Input Data Services Ltd, Bridgwater, Somerset

Printed in Great Britain by Clays Ltd, Elcograf S.p.A.

MIX
Paper from
responsible sources
FSC® C104740
FSC
www.fsc.org

www.orionbooks.co.uk

I dedicate this book to my amazing, fabulous, near and far-reaching family and friends – thank you for believing in me.

Most especially, I would like to dedicate this book to my mother. I hope the little girl you left all those decades ago has managed to make you proud.

And to my wonderful father who had to pick up the pieces.

Contents

CONTENTS

CONTENTS

Prologue

I've dipped in and out of living in the countryside most of my life, but being the type of person who slightly allows life to happen to them, I woke up one morning and found that I seemed to have embedded myself well and truly in London.

So, in 2015, when Graham said, 'Let's move to this farm in Somerset,' I didn't take a great deal of notice of him.

He'd been wibbling on for years about building a house that had all the best bits of our home in Yorkshire, Rise Hall, and all our favourite parts of various other houses we had known and currently knew, but with the added benefit of a farm we could turn into beautiful parkland like the Capability Brown parkland that surrounded Rise.

As lovely as this sounded – and it made for great evening conversations pondering over the perfect this and that about houses – as time went on, and as persuasive as he is, the thought of actually moving lock, stock and barrel to the country just didn't seem feasible to me.

By the time we were having this particular conversation, I had been based in London working a variety of businesses and jobs and developing property one way or another for nearly thirty years. But more than that, we had fourteen years of having four children under our belts, with the network of systems and friends that held all that together. I was also well aware that everything was actually tied together by considerably more fragile threads than I cared to admit . . .

So whenever a farm came up in the country that sparked Graham's imagination, I was happy to humour him by going to take a look as it involved a jolly to the country and we had both always loved looking at properties and land. And anyway, it sort of classed as 'work'.

But honestly, the truth is, I never had any real intention of actually buying a farm. It wasn't just that I knew nothing much about farming, although that felt like a fairly substantial obstacle, but it was also that I had never been that interested in learning about something that seemed to be so very slow.

Mother Nature only had one cycle a year when things happened and that was the best bits – planting and growing some things took years. And that, for an impatient person like me, was just too slow.

And yet, there I was, one wintry morning in the spring of 2018, standing in an enormous barn, in the middle of an enormous farm, taking a delivery of an enormous amount of packing boxes.

A lifetime of our family's belongings arriving at our new home, Graham's aforementioned farm, in Somerset. We didn't have the space to store most of them as the plan was to build our new dream house on the site, but that was all still to come.

Nevertheless, the stuff came. So much of it!

OK, I am a self-confessed hoarder. I have a sentimental attachment to far more things than is either sensible or reasonable. My holy grail is to overcome this failing or 'rebrand' it by having everything either on display – for example, framed and on the wall – or being used.

This means that I get unnecessarily stressed about boxes of unknown 'stuff' lying around – especially if they are all just gathering dust, which much of the content of these boxes we had collected over the last thirty years together definitely were.

Ahead of our move to Somerset I promised myself that I would simplify my life, so here was a good place to start. I would gather the lorry loads of our 'stuff' that had been liberally spread around the country in various homes and projects, put it all together in the barn and simplify that down.

My driving reason for this was that I don't want any of my children to have the burden of having to unburden themselves of the debris of my consumer-filled life.

Graham, a few years ago, had 'bonfire-gate' as I now

like to call it. Along with lots of genuinely unwanted and unrecyclable objects, various things I thought I really wanted (even if I knew they were not actually needed) were destroyed in his purge.

They were some childhood toys of my mother's that were a bit broken but were on my to-do list of things I was, one day perhaps in my retirement or something, going to mend.

He didn't realise their significance and only found out too late. I was furious and so sad, and in my distress I turned, as always, to my excellent counsellors – my kids.

Billy said, 'Why would you want to keep all that stuff anyway?'

I explained that I was going to mend it and then they could have it one day. He looked utterly bemused and asked why he or his children would want it.

Sometimes it takes a child to hold a mirror up to enable you to see the reality of a situation, but in that moment Billy released me from a great deal of the responsibility I felt for the endless 'items' I had accumulated.

You have to be very careful in life to ensure that you don't end up with your belongings owning you rather than the other way around.

The moment your life is governed by housing your items, storing your items, moving your items – then you have to consider whether your items actually own you or you are in possession of them. Even worse, you end up going to work to earn money to pay for the space to store it all!

I recognise that I have been dancing on this fence for most of my life but even with that recognition, it is hard to be as ruthless as I know I logically should be.

But then emotions rarely have much to do with logic. When someone you love very much dies there is a tendency to keep things that remind you of them; it is an unconscious default setting in fear that you might somehow forget them without these trinkets they left behind.

It may be understandable but it's not making your life better or brighter, and it almost certainly is not the legacy that anyone who loved you would want to be leaving behind.

I was once told that possessions and indeed dead bodies are a bit like empty boxes of chocolates. You have all the chocolates inside you as you've eaten them so there is no need for the empty box anymore.

It was a rather lovely piece of advice. It also helped me get over the fact that I've always felt a bit guilty about not going to my mother's funeral despite the fact it was a decision I didn't take, being only ten years old.

Perhaps it explains my obsessive need to hold onto things? Looking around that barn, so many treasures stared back at me – boxes of possessions and furniture that told the story of my life.

Like the scraps of furniture from when Graham and I first met at eighteen and nineteen years old. Stuff that didn't even have the glamorous description of antique. It was all 'second-hand' or 'recycled from the tip' (though I think the fun police of risk assessors and health and safety have knocked that great game on the head now).

Then there was all the stuff from Rise Hall.

From the moment in our late twenties that Graham and I bought that semi-derelict empty stately home, we opened the floodgates and were suddenly the natural home for endless friends and family's 'I don't know what to do with this' pieces of furniture and knick-knacks.

There was also a load of unwanted stuff from my childhood home that my father and stepmother had passed on to me as well as things passed down from mine and Graham's grandparents' home of sixty years that had come our way. Although I must admit we were definitely complicit in effectively becoming an elephant's graveyard for anyone and everyone's belongings as with ninety-seven rooms to furnish we were super grateful for the filler and it came thick and fast.

On top of this came the contents of our London home, which had started as a two-bedroom cottage but ended up being extended to a seven-bedroom family home step by step as baby after baby arrived.

Oh, and not forgetting the contents of our treehouse cabin!

One summer, when Rise Hall was full of weddings and we were camping in one room in our home in London whilst major building work was being under-taken, we bought a few acres in Somerset with a stream, a wood and a small shed we rebuilt as an off-grid tree-house cabin to escape to. It was our little bit of magic in a manic time (though probably better in my head than in reality!).

We sold this field and the cabin too and so had everything we had filled that with as well.

Down it all came.

A couple of shipping containers and one slightly leaky barn later, all our worldly possessions were in one county and in one postcode.

I stared at the lifetime of boxes knowing that inside, every item told a story.

Ever since I was a little girl, my father told me the tale of how he arrived in his first marriage with only a set of broken false teeth and a broken pipe. When I found the false teeth and part of the pipe, I smiled at the memory of his retold story.

I have thrown the teeth away but couldn't quite throw away the pipe, which now sits on a shelf in the downstairs loo – not useful or beautiful but considerably better than the teeth, although equally likely to never be used again.

It would be four years, a pandemic, a terrifying diagnosis and a host of magical adventures involving murderous bees, bird feeding and a very sentimental doll's house, before I finally unpacked the last of those boxes in our beautiful new family home in the country-side.

I

Golden syrup on bread and a goat called Far

I'm not sure exactly what it is about property that I have always found so engaging. I guess it's the perfect blend of history, social history, people, relationships, retail, manufacturing, engineering, dealing and trading that all go into making up the fabric of a building.

Better still, every single building is different, either in its foundations, its construction, its legalities or its planning position.

Certainly, I've always had an insatiable desire to own property and I do know where that comes from – an overwhelming desire to not be told what to do or, as some would like to call it, being a fully qualified control freak!

Ever since I can remember, I wanted to be able to control the environment I was in and the best way to do that was to not only work for myself but also own the roof over my head.

The country has always been in my blood and heart

having had 'sort of' self-sufficient parents but I guess if you looked back, you could possibly chalk it up to something that started soon after my mother died. That first night, my father, older brother Diccon and I dragged a mattress into the spare room and we all slept together in there until the house was sold six months later.

Moving was a fresh start. It meant we didn't have to live in a house with a hole in it in a physical way – emotionally the loss leaves a hole, but at least there were no gaps and empty chairs in rooms that we could visually see.

Our childhood home provided my brother Diccon and I with endless hours of happy adventures. Originally it had been a pair of Victorian workers' cottages on the edge of the Duke of Wellington's estate, Stratfield Saye, in Hampshire, which my parents bought for about £2,000 in 1967. The cottages were semi-derelict and my parents – who we both clearly get our pioneering property spirit from – lived in a caravan in the garden whilst they knocked them together. By the time I came along, they had turned the cottages into a super cool home with four bedrooms and one bathroom.

I was eleven when we left that house but I still remember so much about it. The shelves in my bedroom neatly stacked with toys and books from endless jumble sales (my mother was an inveterate jumble sale goer), the orange and purple swirly wallpaper on the ceiling in the kitchen and the electric blue melamine worktops with purple painted cabinets that my father had built. I don't think you could have had a more 1970s interior if you had tried.

There was also a highly polished oak staircase with square polished spindles and open risers so that if you lay on your front on the landing, you could look through into the kitchen and watch anyone who was in there (albeit they were upside down).

We often used to slip down the stairs if we weren't wearing slippers, which was incredibly painful!

But I loved it all.

Especially the garden. The garden was one of two halves – one immaculately manicured, the other not.

The scruffy garden had a couple of old cars on blocks that my parents used to store clothes my mother had found in jumble sales that didn't yet fit us (I told you she was a veteran jumble sale goer, even collecting bargains for us to use in the future!). I used to sit in those cars, surrounded by bin liners full of clothes, and pretend to drive, tweaking the buttons, switching things on and off and turning the wheel in a way you only do before you actually understand how steering works. The engine may not have worked but I could make those noises so it didn't matter much.

In this half of the garden there was always a 'project' going on – namely my father constructing a shed of some sort, either a new loose box for an animal or to store 'stuff'.

He was once given a totally beautiful wooden caravan with leaded windows and a roof that wound up that needed extensive restoration. I remember being inside its magical interior as a small child and even then I used to dream about fixing it up myself.

Alas it didn't get restored in time. By the time I was old enough to embark on the restoration myself, it had been reclaimed by nature. Literally all that was left was a chassis and pieces of glass.

Sadly I let that one get away. I have never seen a caravan the same since and often wonder if I would be able to recreate it from my memory somehow one day. Clearly I haven't quite let it go after all . . .

The buildings got filled up with this and that. The garage, which was initially built with the house, was used for a car for a short time until it became storage for one of my mother's auction finds – a couple of lorry loads of the component parts for a variety of wooden children's toys.

There were baby-walkers that you put those coloured square blocks in with numbers on, hobby horses, little wooden trikes, doll's cots and dustbin after dustbin of various primary-coloured small balls with holes through them.

I think it was only £100 or so to buy it all, which they did. Then, piece by piece, my father would put together these toys and they would deliver them to various shops for them to sell.

It also meant that as a child I remember these component parts popping up all over the place, like a new knob for the kettle lid or the baby-walker wheels on trolleys to move things about.

Diccon and I would spend time climbing around this garage and digging our hands into the dustbins of smooth varnished balls or clambering around the piles of cot sides.

The house seemed enormous when I myself was a small child but probably wasn't nearly as big as I remember, proving life is all relative!

At its heart was a temperamental, old, cream Rayburn that my father would fill with logs. This was used to heat the water and cook on, although as it regularly went out, food was often pretty late and sometimes raw.

I don't remember very regular meals – there was generally one proper meal a day but the other meals depended on whether my mother or father were catering. If it was my father, then meals tended to involve salad cream on bread for the main course and then golden syrup on bread for pudding. Or sometimes sardines on toast.

If it was my mother, it would be dried fruit, which she bought in massive sacks from a wholesaler, along with some chopped carrots.

We both preferred our father's meals!

My parents' holy grail was self-sufficiency, which is nigh on impossible to achieve but we certainly grew and picked the carrots and all the other fruit and vegetables ourselves for our irregular dinners.

This required a considerable amount of digging – my mother was insistent that everything was double dug, which involved turning the soil over and then over again to break it up. I believe it was considered the best way at the time to make the best soil for growing things and was certainly hard work.

I do look back and think the produce from the garden couldn't possibly have justified the number of hours spent embedded in compost with a near-permanent layer of dirt under one's fingernails, but then when you are a child I don't think you tend to question things around you, your normality is what is there.

Diccon's and my contributions were not always helpful even though we did have the best of intentions. Once we dug a large and muddy duck pond in the middle of the manicured lawn for a pair of ducks that we had incubated in the downstairs loo.

We spent quite a lot of time up trees, in particular the Victoria plum where we always ate far too much of the fruit far too early and made ourselves ill. We also spent a lot of time hiding in the raspberry canes scouring them for their ruby goodies.

We were relatively feral with few rules and non-existent bedtimes, although every now and then when my father had clearly had enough he would take the fuse out of the upstairs lights to try and keep us in bed.

Alas this didn't work very well as we quickly learnt to claim to be 'scared of the dark' and used this excuse to bounce out of bed again.

There were lots of animals in that house – ducks, seven goats, a dog, a fat ginger cat and a very muddy and unbrushed pony called Bracken who I brought into the kitchen on a regular basis.

The goats got pregnant (somehow!) and gave birth. We were scooped out of bed one night at three o'clock in the morning to come and watch, which I do remember as being amazing but mainly because we ate macaroni cheese afterwards, which was my absolute favourite.

The goats, or at least our biggest goat, Far, was also the source of one of the most embarrassing episodes of my childhood when my parents decided to bring her into my school to show the other children how she was milked.

It was a fairly stuffy all-girls private school in the middle of Reading. My parents, wanting the best for me, moved heaven and earth to send me there, hocking themselves into debt and living a very frugal life indeed to be able to meet the fees.

An array of smart company cars and drivers used to deliver their charges at the beginning and end of the day. My parents had a very old and very dented brown Renault 5.

On this particular day they somehow managed to ram our very large goat Far into the boot of it and out they got in their muddy wellies and scruffy gardening gear, fashioning themselves more on Tom and Barbara from *The Good Life* than Jerry and Margo, who would have fitted in rather better.

Every window looking out over the immaculately groomed lawn had faces pressed up against them as all classes got a bird's eye view of the unusual scene: my parents leading our goat onto the lawn armed with a milking stool and a tin bucket.

My class had been led out to the lawn itself for the up close and personal experience by our Miss Honey type of joyous, young and enthusiastic class teacher. My parents milked Far, who then proceeded to kick over the bucket of milk and poo on the croquet pitch-quality lawn.

There were many horrified faces as well as a lot of giggling before the headmistress appeared with a face like thunder and 'equipment' for my parents to remove what the goat had gifted the lawn and icy glares for our teacher who had clearly not run this animal escapade past her boss.

It was an early lesson in resilience, as if I could have teleported out of there I would have done. I can still picture the dozens of laughing faces at all the windows.

I didn't stay long at that school, although not because of 'poo-gate'. It was because of Mr Fish.

Mr Fish was a joyous older man who lived next door to us. He worked at Thames Water and must have been very senior because he had a jolly smart car and he was persuaded to give me lifts to school.

He also sometimes took me back to his house after school, where he and his smiley wife, Mrs Fish, would give me chocolate biscuits. (This is not the only reason I liked them by the way.)

Anyway, Mr Fish had to leave for work earlier than would have been ideal, but the school was meant to be open at that time so it shouldn't have been a problem. After a month or two of this arrangement, however, my parents discovered that the school wasn't actually open and I, aged four, had been standing on the pavement for half an hour on my own.

Understandably, in my opinion, they were a little peeved with the school. The headmistress, already not a big fan of mine, got into trouble for her long breakfasts at home and whether it was the goat's poo or the time-keeping, who knows, but my parents decided to enrol me in a closer and more rural school.

I didn't mind that school so much – I can't say that I had a ball but it wasn't an entirely negative environment.

I had a maths teacher called Mr Doran who had a moustache like Magnum, P.I., whom I thought very handsome. He had a habit of pulling up his grey slacks with the sides of his thumbs whilst holding chalk between his thumb and forefinger which I thought a very cool trick.

As a result, I listened intently in maths and was

9

therefore very good with numbers and top of the class. Sadly, he left to do a management training course at Marks and Spencer (I have never really forgiven M&S) and my grades took a rapid decline from then on. One of my missed careers was engineering, which stupidly and sadly starts and stops with your ability in maths at an early age. I would have loved to be an engineer.

When I left this school I went on to a secondary girls' boarding school that could only very loosely be called an educational establishment. I really hated boarding – my mother had just died and I didn't want to be at school, and I certainly didn't want to be boarding there. My beloved brother was at a boarding school elsewhere and I longed for us all to be together just *somewhere* else.

I couldn't relate to any of the teachers, most of whom were single older ladies without family or a sense of humour (or at least that's how they all seemed to me). I did have one English teacher I liked who taught drama and put on a play whilst I was there, but she was considered a bit 'out there'.

I remember my first history lesson when I started studying O levels (yes, I am that old to have caught the last year of them), I was given an A4 sheet of white paper with a long list of dates and events next to them.

This, I was told, was what we would be learning for the next two years. Homework was to learn the list by the next lesson. I now know that the ONLY boring part of history is the dates so it is unfathomable that a teacher would start there. I didn't listen in history again for the next two years.

Somehow I managed to leave school knowing quite literally nothing about twentieth-century history or either world war (including their dates) and achieved a U for Ungraded in the examination.

I think it is fair to say that school and I didn't agree with each other very well. It wasn't that I was particularly naughty, it's just that I couldn't really see any *point* in learning. School to me was just serving time until I could legally leave and get on with life. I think I wasn't a big fan of being told what to do and most of the rules at school seemed to me not to have particularly good reasons for being set.

So I applied to a local sixth-form college to study drama on a foundation course, which was much more up my street. I took this along with English (I hadn't managed to pass my O level but fortunately they didn't check my grade and I certainly didn't volunteer the information) and art.

Sixth-form college definitely suited me better – there seemed more point to the teachers and being a student, and more relevancy to what we were learning. I liked the fact there were boys and girls there and male and female teachers, and they were all less peculiar and actually seemed quite interested in the subjects they were teaching.

But still, learning things to me was just wasting time that I could be spending getting on with life in the big bad world of endless possibilities out there. I had literally NO intention of going on to study anything else.

Looking back now, I recognise that my relationship with the written word was always a bumpy one. My four sons were all one by one diagnosed with dyslexia, I however was diagnosed with being 'uncooperative' at school. It's just possible that I may be dyslexic too.

Their father, who is undoubtedly very talented indeed in the arts in all its guises, was not particularly academic either and, with apples never falling that far from the tree, it's probably not that surprising that our children are 'reluctant readers' at best!

What I do know is that when I walked out of my last A level exam and everyone around me was talking about what they had written about and how they thought they had done, I only had one thought as I walked down the steps: 'As long as I live, I will never ever sit another exam.'

The sense of freedom was overwhelming – the sky was blue and I was so very excited to be free to start the rest of my life.

And buy my first house.

2

Living in a van and estate agents in ill-fitting suits

I've always loved camping. But then again I've had lots of practice of sleeping in slightly odd places.

After we sold the family home, my father moved us into a caravan. But it was pretty small and turning the beds into a seating area and back daily was time-consuming and complicated, so after about a week my father, Diccon and I slept in the little space in the eaves above the single garage, which at the time seemed like a great adventure.

My father had kept the garage and a chunk of the land, and set about building us another home on the land next door to our old home. So whilst this was going on, we lived between the caravan during the day and at night climbed a ladder that led up through a hole in the ceiling of the garage into the space above where three mattresses just about fitted.

I've always been mad about cats and my father was pretty weak in stopping me from collecting new kittens from a friend who lived on a farm nearby.

My new cat was very skilled at climbing the vertical ladder as well as sort of falling/jumping down it, which I considered very cool indeed. One night we went up and found she had given birth in Diccon's bed (my father hadn't noticed she was pregnant and I didn't really connect her fat stomach to kittens). It made the whole adventure even more exciting, though Diccon and I had to share my mattress for a bit! I have later discovered that when you get on well with animals they tend to give birth in your bed, which I take to be a compliment about your relationship more than a dirty protest!

In many ways things were pretty unsettled after my mother died, though my father did what he had to do to make ends meet and provide us with everything we needed and whilst it may have been a bit unconventional, the three of us were incredibly close.

My first stepmother, who we called Boo, came along when I was twelve and was brilliant in so many ways. But in quick succession our mother had died, we left our home and moved into a garage and a caravan (admittedly in the field next door so not that far), my father had remarried, and my brother went to boarding school, and then I went off to a different boarding school, leaving my father and stepmother to finish building our new home together.

Watching a lonely broken father grieving is more painful than you can imagine. I learnt at that tender young age that witnessing someone you love in pain is worse than dealing with your own.

A child's perspective on most things is often morphed out of reality – after all, everyone sees the world though their own lens – but when I look back, I know that I spent a goodly amount of my childhood labouring under the illusion that I could somehow 'fix' some of the tougher moments I could see others I loved going through.

Of course, now I can see how absurd most of those thoughts were, but nevertheless it doesn't stop a child from *feeling* they are responsible.

That sense of responsibility carries with it a rich topping of guilt and those deep-seated emotions are hard to shake off.

But by the time I left sixth form my father had been married to Boo for some years and together they had finished building the house and created a new garden around it.

I no longer felt he needed caring for in the same way and I therefore felt less responsible for him. It was time to concentrate on finding somewhere to live myself.

Obviously a house, even a flat, was out of the question – there was no way I could afford one. I couldn't even afford what seemed to me the next best thing – a motorhome.

So I settled for a van. An ex-local-authority Simca van to be exact which, by the time it came to me had previously been owned by a couple of builders so it came complete with an awful lot of rubble.

I bought it with the £200 my father had kindly given me for my eighteenth birthday and I could not have been more excited.

I scrubbed the back out and filled it with a few layers of old underlay, carpet and cushions. I also painted the bonnet and sides with flames and the words 'Greased Lightning' in a predicable lightning bolt. An act of stupidity that did nothing more than earn me a goodly number of well-deserved driving points mainly for drawing unnecessary attention to myself whilst attempting to tell the world (that wasn't interested anyway) how sensationally individual I was.

Points aside, that van really was brilliant fun. It had no windows in the sides and I, not being very tall, could perfectly fit in the back. Being a bit of a bed snob, I wasn't a fan of laying on the hallway floor to sleep at a party and so instead I had my lovely warm duvet and pillows all ready for me wherever I was.

And so, armed with my van and my father's advice to 'know your capital city', like Dick Whittington I set off for London.

Living in a van in London had its precarious moments. I had to go to garages to use the loo and I rarely arrived at someone's flat without asking if I might be able to have a quick bath or shower.

And in the winter it was jolly cold. The van steamed up overnight so there would be terrible condensation in the morning, which sometimes froze. On those days I would generally find an accommodating friend I could go and stay with!

But for the most part I was very happy.

Even so, the lure of a home with its own walls and a roof tugged away at me. The fact that I didn't actually have the money to buy one I chose to regard not as a barrier but rather a hurdle that merely needed overcoming. I started to spend an awful lot of time staring in estate agents' windows.

There were endless agents willing to help, especially when I said the word 'unmodernised'. At that point all sorts of exciting possibilities would come flying out of their filing cabinets.

Even more possibilities materialised when, having realised that by limiting your budget to somewhere near affordable you didn't ever get to see the really juicy properties, I upped my budget from £50,000 to an entirely imaginary £500,000.

Suddenly I was viewing blocks of flats and eight-bedroom town houses. Remember this was the late 1980s and no one wanted to buy property. Markets had just had a meteoric crash and interest rates were in double figures, and anyone who was anyone was obsessed with Silicon Valley.

This new digital world had arrived like an extra-terrestrial spaceship bringing with it a new language that seemed as far-fetched as the sci-fi films I had never understood why anyone watched.

But a building? A building was tangible. It had walls and a roof – and I was busy being shown around all manner of properties whilst clutching endless sets of printed paper sales particulars.

I could see potential everywhere. I have never been very good at knowing limitations – to me everything is possible, it's just a case of how you get around a problem.

Buildings have never been any different. The bigger the building or the bigger the problem, the harder you have to think about how to overcome it. In fact, I think I slightly get a kick out of having a bigger problem to overcome.

And besides, in those days, it was all hypothetical anyway. I was only ever imagining what I might do without having to actually commit and be responsible for the outcome.

But as time went on, never *actually* seeing through these daydreams became more and more frustrating. I was desperate to just get on with 'doing' something rather than just talking about it.

I needed to earn some money.

Estate agents

Back then estate agents were like different species to the ones we know now.

There were a few types. You'd get the estate agents that had set themselves up in a shop they had almost certainly bought – in much of London in those days, shops had no real capital value so you'd often get the shop chucked in for free with the residential flats above. This was because it didn't stack up to run a business there if the shops cost a lot to buy or rent, especially when the rates and bills were high.

These estate agents had dirty windows, a shop sign that had aged as much as the agent himself, and an interior 'shop fit' that was little more than a pot of brilliant white paint chucked fairly badly on top of the old interior. It was never quite enough to disguise the previous use of the space as a failed hairdresser/corner shop/cafe.

The pictures in the window of houses for sale (which was the only way to advertise the properties available apart from the newspaper, which was an expensive marketing tool) had been on display so long the colours had been bleached out of them by the sun.

I learnt there was rarely much point in entering these offices as they were glorified spaces for the occupier to carry out another line of work rather than an agency selling or developing homes.

Next there were the proper independent estate agents, or sometimes independents with two or three branches. These were the best because they tended to be owned by one person who worked there (generally a man), who had started the business and had a vision for creating a really brilliant agency.

They had invested in their branding and signage, they had invested in their shop fit and they seemed to invest in their staff too. They were generally happy places with people working there who were sometimes only passing through on their career path or sometimes there for the long term, but they were keen to be successful and good at what they did.

Staff had people skills and a good understanding of the commodity they were selling. They also were generally fun and helpful, driven enough to channel their undoubted selling skills into something more interesting and engaging than door-to-door sales but perhaps not hungry enough to be on a trading floor.

A few years later when the internet started taking off, it was these smaller independents that were often sucked up into much larger investment bodies that owned large swathes of the estate agency market (under all the various little brands) and bought out. Those canny owners took the cash offers on the table at just the right time, retiring happily to pastures new.

This market, much like most others, has been 'disrupted' by the internet, but just like many other things that have been disrupted by the internet it has definitely not yet settled into the perfect PI (post-internet) model that works well enough to be the 'new norm'.

The biggest problem with the internet is the very thing

I love most about property. Buildings are always, always different and their occupants are always, always different. Whether people are living or working or shopping or making something inside a building, you will, I am somewhat joyously delighted to say, NEVER get the same circumstances.

But then there came a new breed of residential estate agent who were none of the above. Whilst there were still 'deal makers' and commercial agents with a lot of experience, knowledge and surveying qualifications, these new agents didn't have any of the aforementioned skills or experience.

These are the ones who have given plenty of fodder for comedians and sketch shows ever since: namely wide-boy salesmen with lots to say and no knowledge all delivered in a badly fitting suit.

3

Golden Grahams and my
very first flat

My employment CV is varied and totally disjointed. The first summer job I had was when I was thirteen and was in Wellington Country Park in the days when thirteen-year-olds were allowed to work at weekends and in their school holidays. I worked in the shop behind the till before being moved to the ice-cream counter.

The ice cream was made by the estate (which was quite radically unusual in those days, when everyone else was just selling Zooms, strawberry splits or Mr Whippys) and came in hazelnut crunch, mint choc chip, strawberry, mango, coffee and chocolate. (I am sooo impressed with myself for remembering all those flavours thirty-plus years later!!)

I enjoyed the work in spite of being called into the manager's office for a ticking off after giving a kindly looking older couple an extra free scoop – it turned out they were the Duke and Duchess of Wellington, who weren't so grateful for me issuing my largesse on them, what with it being on their bill!

Despite this, over years of on and off work there, I was eventually promoted onto the ice-cream bicycle, which meant that I could set up stall wherever I fancied around the large lake – much more appealing to me.

I also worked in the cafe where I honed my skills at flipping burgers and cooking frozen chips. I was never going to win awards for my burger and chips but as far as I am aware I didn't poison anyone, so I'd call this a success!

You didn't need any paperwork to run a cafe in those days so I was pretty free to do as I wanted and a few years later when I could drive even offered to do the Cash-and-Carry run, getting a weird kick from choosing things that customers might want to buy.

Moonlighting from this job, I also worked at a Little Chef as I could easily reach it on my bike. I washed up there and learnt two things – one was how to use an industrial dishwasher; which I was thrilled to discover only took three minutes to run (very satisfying if you are trying to get through a lot of plates quickly). The second was that I didn't want to work at the Little Chef for long. The manager, who was not a very nice lady and reminded me of one of the teachers at my boarding school, had been there for years. Obviously not literally as she went home at night – but I knew then I needed something more than that out of life. It made me think of one of my favourite books, which is *Oh, the Places*

You'll Go! by Dr. Seuss. Graham finds it annoying as he says you can't just make up words when you can't find one that rhymes, which admittedly the author did a lot – but if you want inspiration for life you need to read it anyway.

Also available by my bike was a local conference centre where my brother started as a cleaner going around the loos, was promoted onto changing beds and cleaning, then to pot washer and then was trained in silver service waiting. I followed his career path there and have found in particular silver service waiting a very useful addition to my basket of so-called qualifications. It has the added bonus of meaning I can endlessly be 'right' in conversations with my children about all things related to table manners and table laying.

On top of this I started a couple of businesses. One was a window cleaning business, which was born from the fact that I had an ex-local authority van with a fixed roof rack. This business turned out not to be long lived for various tedious reasons I won't bore you with.

The other was a sandwich round in our local village – not massively successful either as there were always a lot of sandwiches left over so the balance sheet didn't fully stack up. I'm also not at all sure my health and safety would have stood up to an inspection of any sort though I am pleased to say that there were no complaints!

I think all this time I had this feeling that if you just

kept on trying something would turn out right, but ultimately I wanted to earn my own money.

After this I got my first 'proper' job working for a chartered surveyor.

My father had been keen for me to complete a secretarial course; it was a 'bit of a deal' of him agreeing he would support me going to drama school, which I kept on applying to though never actually got offered a place. So I did a three-month course in Bournemouth between finishing my A levels and heading for London.

Bournemouth seemed the best option as a) the course had both sexes and all ages. Lots of secretarial colleges were only for girls who were straight out of school and I wasn't sure I liked the idea of spending that much time with all school-leaver girls, who seemed rather terrifying, as well as having to learn to type and do shorthand.

And b) it was a crammer course of twelve weeks so would be over far quicker. I was desperate to get it all over and done with as quickly as possible, so this suited me down to the ground.

I found a room to rent in the *Loot* newspaper (which is how you found rooms to rent in the days before the internet) phoned them from a call box, viewed it and agreed to take it. A week later I moved into a room in a house with a strange guy who owned it and another casual renter in another room who was working on a fishing boat. I didn't use the house much – I was either out or eating Pot Noodles in my room.

The minute those twelve weeks were over, I headed to London armed with my secretarial course cert and not-very-many-words-a-minute shorthand, and secured my first job at a chartered surveyors.

It didn't last long.

I am not sure the man who I worked for really needed a shorthand secretary as he told me to 'take a pen', and then just marched up and down his office with his hands behind his back dictating a thank you letter to his granny!

I tried, and failed, to get a job as a trainee manager at John Lewis but did land a job in the Save the Children's appeals department, where I learnt a lot about the charity sector and, as luck would have it, met a dear life-long friend.

At the same time I took on pub work and also had various stints doing nannying and babysitting, where I discovered that some children are delicious and some are perfectly ghastly – largely their parents followed their traits (or is it the other way around?!).

I have, over the years, often thought of the children and parents I met and have met since, and I am certain I have learnt one thing: if a child is hideous and their parents are gorgeous – it's a phase they'll grow out of. If a child is hideous and their parents are also hideous, it is a permanent affectation that will last a lifetime. I have rarely been wrong about this.

But even with all these endless jobs on top of various day jobs and a colourfully creative CV of my finances, I still wasn't in a position to buy a property. But then something else changed: I met my now husband, Graham.

My brother Diccon, who had at the time just finished at The University of London studying economics and philosophy, told me he had a new girlfriend and that I'd really like her brother. I thought he was being rather irritating and certainly had absolutely no intention of speaking to or even meeting this random man.

Then a few weeks later, Diccon, who was running a decorating business at the time, rang to ask for my help finishing a job he had painting the stairs at a block of flats in Pimlico. When I turned up, Graham was also working there, and to my chagrin, I reluctantly came to realise he was actually really cool.

I gave him a lift home at the end of the day and when we pulled up at some traffic lights, I asked him to jump out and buy me some flowers.

He opened the door, jumped out and two minutes later jumped back in with a huge grin and passed the bouquet to me. To be honest he had me there and then, though I'd never admit this to him. He was and still is impulsive and unpredictable and I love that.

Two days after meeting, Graham suggested I moved in with him – into a room he was renting on a week-by-week basis in Streatham.

Somehow wherever we lived was a good deal more fun with the two of us. In fact, everything became more fun when I met him. We ate a lot of Golden Grahams (mainly because they are delicious and not because of the name, though it did make us snigger), and dreamt up all sorts of schemes for our future together.

Not long after that, we left the slightly depressing room in Streatham and fell back on my cosy van. Adventures in our home on wheels were many, and the freedom it brought to have your home with you wherever you went was a point of luxury enough to counterbalance the mild inconvenience of having no bathroom or kitchen.

So now there were two of us and, along with Diccon, our business plans now had the three of us. Finally, after window shopping for property of all shapes and sizes for nearly two years, we bought an unmodernised one-and-a-half bedroomed ground-floor flat on a road in Battersea with no bathroom, condemned electrics and an outside loo for £52,000.

I was nineteen years old and felt very grown up indeed.

4

Rising damp, French drains and a building control officer called Mr Gubby

Buying the flat was a massive stretch financially. At the time, no one we knew was earning double figures and so with normal salaries around six or seven thousand a year we had to be pretty creative, but in those days you could find a mortgage broker who had far less checks and balances than there are now.

Their job was to sell mortgages and we were happy and willing customers. You massaged things here and there and prayed you'd be able to keep all your jobs to meet the repayments.

I can't tell you how overwhelmingly exciting that very first completion day was. There are moments when I think it might be interesting to dig deep to understand more about why it mattered so much to me but then there is a danger you unroot something that simply isn't there. Certainly there was an element of 'making a home' involved.

With my father now happily remarried and me now

being the proud owner of a key to a front door I had bought with my two best friends, life was about as good as it could be.

The interior of the flat, however, left much to be desired. Once inside, the smell of damp hit you immediately and the place was covered in mildew and black mould, but nothing could knock us off our happy perch. It was ours.

We found an assortment of glasses in different shapes and sizes at a charity shop, bought a bottle of wine and revelled in the moment – we owned our own four walls and we could do whatever we wanted within them. We could have a double bed and share it, we could smoke cigarettes inside, we could invite whoever we wanted over whenever we wanted and eat Pot Noodles for breakfast.

I also loved the thought of getting letters through the letter box addressed to us. I loved the independence and probably ultimately the control.

Every room of the tiny flat was a grown-up version of the camps that my brother and I spent our childhood building in the woods, or the dens we made in holes in the haystacks at my friend's farm.

My father came up to London, bringing with him the gift of his old hand drill and a few ideas on where we should start. He was a building surveyor by trade but always practised as an architect so was a godsend.

He originally worked for Bovis when he left college.

When I was a child, he always pointed out Marks & Spencer in Reading and I was completely in awe, assuming he had built it single-handedly. He came a little off the high pedestal when I was older and realised in reality he was a site manager there at some point.

My father pointed us in the right direction for the flat renovation and the three of us set quickly to work. We learnt fast.

First up we blocked up the door to the garden so that we could convert that corridor space into a bathroom. This involved blockwork, which we knew how to do as we had mixed up mortar for our father many times at home.

The internal plasterwork had blown and needed replacing, so we set about hacking it off the walls (well, actually, it didn't need much hacking as most of it fell off).

We learnt about rising damp and French drains and moisture transference and the different methods of retrofitting a damp proof course and how they worked or were meant to work.

We learnt about building regulations and building control and how you work out the structure of how a building stays up and what on earth an RSJ (reinforced steel joist) was.

We then met Mr Gubby, our local authority building control officer (before the days of privatisation of building control when all the brains and experience were still at the local authority). He was amazing, an avuncular figure who couldn't have been more supportive. He was utterly pragmatic and never left us without having come up with a solution to whatever problem we were going through.

We also met a wonderful elderly structural engineer called Leo who knew almost everything there was to know about building and anything he didn't immediately know he was always able to work out within a day.

I realised then that there are two types of people in the world: those who create problems and those who solve them. You have to decide which one you want to be as it's more of a state of mind than any reflection of your existing abilities. Those who solve problems are, to be honest, more fun to be around.

Without having these amazing problem-solvers in the early days we certainly would not have ended up with the businesses we did.

One of the biggest jobs was knocking the sitting room into the hallway to make it bigger. First we had to put an RSJ in to stop the flat above ending up in our flat. We put it in over a weekend as my brother was by this time working full-time for a graphic design company, I was working at Save the Children and Graham, who had a better relationship with education than I did, had started university studying art. Graham's painting and drawing didn't really start to take off properly until about ten years later though, when he decided to really commit to it more. I often wonder about his work, which is truly beautifully executed and telling in its subject matter of much deeper thought than I think he is comfortable letting on. The truth, it seems to me, is that like many successful artists, his work doesn't make him happy but it makes him happier than not doing it!

Once the steel was in place and the concrete set and checked, the next weekend was taking the wall out – a far messier job than I had anticipated as knocking out the brickwork released huge clouds of dust that covered everything in our makeshift bedroom in the front room.

Unperturbed, we bagged up all the rubble and carried it out to my van to take it to the dump – much cheaper than getting a skip with a licence.

The next job was to take a window out of the sitting room and replace it with French doors. Since blocking up the back door to build the bathroom, we had to climb out of the window to get to the only loo – which was outside. The new bathroom hadn't been plumbed yet. The French doors meant finally we could easily get outside, which was joyous!

With the new layout of the flat completed, it then all needed plastering and we managed to find a plasterer from a building site down the road who could do a bit of moonlighting with us.

Finally we had to do the plumbing and the electrics, and again we found a plumber and electrician from local building sites. They agreed to do it for a good price so long as we laid most of the cable and pipework ourselves.

This probably all makes it sound easier than it was. We definitely made mistakes.

We learnt that if you don't have the mix of the render (the sand and cement mix that you smooth over blockwork internally or externally to make it flat and watertight) right, it is very hard indeed to get it to stay on a block wall.

Then, once the walls were complete, there were problems with the wallpaper as I didn't soak it for long enough. By the next morning it had so many bubbles behind it that it looked like an Aero bar.

I tried using a syringe to inject the bubbles with paste and roll them flat again. I also tried using a sharp blade to cut them and then tried gluing and rolling them flat but still the bubbles showed. I have never not soaked wallpaper long enough since.

We also had to grasp the rudimentary principles of plumbing pretty quickly. Namely how a combination boiler works and the different types of hot water and heating systems.

But with all these things we were keen learners and it was fun figuring it all out together. Also, everything keeps changing so you have to keep on learning.

There was also the issue of budget – we only had £5,000 to do all the work. We didn't have enough cash for a smart new kitchen or bathroom but managed to find both second-hand. We bought tiles that were reduced because they were end of line and when it came to furnishings everything had been used before too.

We scoured small ads and car-boot sales and were very pleased with our first purchase which was a second-hand double bed that we bought for the princely sum of £5. The idea of a second-hand bed may not be very appealing but actually it isn't that different to sleeping in a hotel bed when you think about it. However, I did splash out on a new mattress cover.

Then with that, our newly renovated flat was complete. We put it back on the market and were utterly thrilled when we sold it for £72,000. Our property business was up and running.

It had taken seven months of hard work but largely we'd really enjoyed it. It was fun learning and working together – even at 2 a.m. in the morning it was fun. We had a local takeaway called Natty Tattys that sold baked potatoes, which was our staple supper throughout that first project.

Diccon slightly cheated by staying a lot with his girlfriend Caroline (Graham's sister) – understandably as she had hot running water! – but even so this was an adventure shared by us all and any adventure shared is so, so much more fun.

Working and spending time with people you love and who make you laugh is surely living the dream, because if you have that it never really feels like work – it's just 'doing something' and when you aren't a big fan of 'doing nothing' then it's all round pretty fab!

From halfway through the project, I was already out and about looking for our next one. There were some really lovely tiny little almshouses in a small estate a short walk away, many of which were for sale, and I set my heart on us doing one of those next.

We found one that was completely unmodernised, again with an outside loo, but this time we had a first floor to play with. We squeezed up the mortgage and agreed on a further re-mortgage when works had been done to make it 'habitable' so we could fund the rest of the work.

Habitable or not, we moved in as soon as we had bought it – and this time with a bit of experience under our belts, we were able to embark on the next project with a little more confidence.

We used our basic RSJ knowledge and we engaged the subcontractors we had built a relationship with, plus a few we hadn't. We extended to the side this time and took down a chimney breast. We replaced the roof, replumbed, rewired, replastered, redecorated and about six months later had it finished.

This is when we knew we would be doing this as a business. We all decided to commit to more risk and more work, and began diversifying our management across several projects at the same time.

Money was always tight, but we were very, very careful with it – as much as was humanly possible was reinvested, and we had low costs and paid ourselves very little. It helped that we were young and didn't need much – an Asda Big Red Wine Box was a perfectly good enough evening's entertainment for us!

I think there is something both learnt over the years but also instinctive that can make you see a property and instantly know how it could be better. Occasionally we were a bit stuck but with three heads we generally came up with a dramatic yet simple solution to make the most of our projects.

5

Disagreements and the 4 a.m. worry

There were most definitely disagreements. Like the day I wanted to change the front door and Diccon and Graham didn't. I got a bee in my bonnet about us having to have a Victorian front door and they felt that the flat-panelled one already there would do, even if it wasn't entirely in keeping with the property.

I changed it anyway without them. They were cross, but I still claim that's why the property sold so quickly – they still claim it was a waste of money, but we'll never know who was right!

There was also the time Diccon and Graham were watching an important football match on a minuscule portable TV on site and I wanted them to screw all the floorboards down as the carpets were being fitted the next day. They showed no sign of moving and amused themselves with ignoring me and saying they'd do it later. Impatient and furious (and to be honest not very interested in the football match), I got on and did it myself, and proceeded to drill through a live pipe! I put my finger on it for a while but eventually had to admit to it and shout to them. They came and drained the system and we repaired the damage I had caused – making them in the right and me in the wrong, which was even more infuriating!

Another memorable drainage moment (the glamour!) was the time one of our flats had a blocked drain and the only way we could work out how to unblock it was to cut through the waste pipe. The only snag was that it was at head height and when we cut into it, Diccon, Graham and I were all underneath. This alone is a very good reason why no one should flush wet wipes down a loo, as if there aren't enough reasons already!

We had deadlines (generally arbitrarily set by me) but we met them regardless of how little sleep we got. At other times we'd have all projects finished and on the market with time to spare. Then we would be able to go out on 'jollies', as we called them, looking at interesting and unusual properties coming up for sale in an auction or that we'd heard about on the grapevine along with other developments.

A property with its future use up for grabs is so intoxicating. I find reinvention exciting, largely because you have boundaries to work within. Without these, building our new home in Somerset was all the more daunting for me as there were so few physical constraints (albeit there were the obvious ones of budget and planning).

In the past we had generally worked within the confines of a small space or site, or piece of land at the end of a row of other buildings, but with roads around and services three feet away under the pavement.

Reinventing a building makes you think hard and work hard, but in so many ways it's almost easier solving a problem when you have an issue to address rather than trying to work out what the problem is you need to solve.

Better still, your experiences colour your judgement. You can draw on what you have learnt already, putting errors behind you but also learning something new every day.

The saying that 'the harder people work the more successful they seem to be' might not be very popular, but it is tricky to disprove. Being self-employed appealed to me though as I did feel in charge of my own destiny, and I learnt you can push yourself to achieve more if you want to. Risk may be risky, but doing nothing is certain to result in nothing. As our lovely solicitor said on one particularly hairy deal when I asked him if he thought we were mad: 'fate favours the bold'.

As long as you have the tools to dust yourself down when things don't go according to plan and then learn from it, which gets easier with time, then you probably can work harder and get further, though it all slightly depends on what the goal is in the first place! After all, we all need to enjoy the journey as the destination is the end.

The risks we have taken have definitely made it an adrenaline-fuelled ride. Debt piled up higher than we could manage, deadlines were sometimes missed, sales occasionally fell through and there were always, always unexpected costs.

One particularly tense moment came when we had several sites running and our bank manager was made redundant. It turned out our debts hadn't been set up how the bank would have liked them and they decided to close all our accounts. Luckily our amazing solicitor pointed out to the bank the error of their ways and it continued to fund the cash flow that had been verbally agreed until the various deals had sold a couple of months later.

There were so many nights I stayed awake worrying about everything we were juggling but I now have learnt some tools to help compartmentalise the 4 a.m. worry.

It ALWAYS seems worse than it is at that time. It is NEVER able to be fixed at that time of night. And everything ALWAYS works out in the end. And if it hasn't worked out yet, then it's not the end. And this is what I tell myself over and over again if I ever wake at 4 a.m.

The flipside to all this worry is that a busy life keeps you about as far away from bored that you can get.

Graham says I've always been in a hurry to get things done. He does have a point. Maybe there is a bit of attention deficit disorder that lurks within or maybe I'm simply in a hurry because I knew my mother didn't live past thirty-nine. Or perhaps I am just plain greedy.

Whatever it is, I am impatient and eager to get on with things. Mix that with someone who doesn't need much sleep and I'm probably quite hard to live with as I juggle thousands of things at the same time and slightly *need* new excitements around every corner to avoid feeling stagnant.

I sometimes wonder what it would be like to be able to just 'be'. To just 'stand still' and enjoy life. But I don't think that is very visible in my DNA. I'm also not 100 per cent sure I want it to be there anyway.

6

Why are we Brits obsessed with owning a home?

In this country I'm not alone in my fascination with the concept of 'home'.

But what is it that drives our national obsession with owning property, rather than renting? After all, ultimately a house is just a tool for living in – it loses its relevance once people aren't in it.

You only need to look at how quickly Mother Nature takes back a building if is unused, and the struggle the National Trust/English Heritage/Churches Conservation Trust have to maintain unused buildings, to know that it's the people inside that is the pulse that keeps them alive.

We live in a country where shelter is more important than some other countries, simply because it's cold and rains a lot so having a roof over your head is pretty essential. But it's not just that; it goes far, far deeper.

It wasn't so long ago that you weren't entitled to vote unless you were an Esquire – meaning you needed to 'own' property. You therefore didn't really have a voice without owning a home. I personally think this helps to underwrite a lot of our sentiment. But there are other factors too. The massive rise in house prices since the war has commoditised our homes.

There is a big conversation to have about what social housing is for. Is it a) a short-term stopgap or is it b) a long-term solution to plug the gap between what we pay our key workers and how much market rents cost.

Then there was the 'privatisation' of social housing, launched with the 'Right to Buy' scheme in the 1980s. This was a scheme that enabled council tenants to purchase their council home with a discount calculated at how many years they had been paying rent there for. Great for tenants who had been there for decades as they could buy their home for next to nothing. As soon as their purchase went through they were then entitled to sell the property and keep the difference. I personally believe the scheme was in many ways an acceptance that the state was going to close up shop and wash their hands of being responsible for where and how people lived. The vague suggestion that the monies would be spent on building new local authority homes was a hollow promise at best.

If the scheme wasn't intended to generate a bit of short-term revenue but largely cut future costs, then we would have kept our council houses for future generations to benefit from and the cash equivalent could have been given to people living in council houses for them to go and buy a property elsewhere. If the goal was to give lumps of cash to long-term council tenants this would have been a less damaging way to do it.

I have literally no idea why any government felt it was entitled to sell our great-grandchildren's council homes off any more than they were entitled to sell our great-grandchildren's school playing fields.

Nevertheless, they did – the result being that *some* people benefitted and that is the only silver lining in the whole plan; but at what cost?

Interestingly, the first-ever couple who took part in 'Right to Buy' split up due to the stress of having a mortgage, but many people did benefit financially. Roughly half of the properties sold through the scheme though are now rented out with tenants paying more than twice the levels charged by local authorities.

I do see the difficulty in choosing whether it is best for any service to be private or state-owned – either option has its downsides and upsides and you could argue for one or the other until you were blue in the face whilst also being correct.

It's a balance of probability based on the human being and how it behaves that I think leads you to the best solution.

So on the one hand the principle for privatisation is an easy one to agree with – avoid the absurd waste and systems for systems' sake and jobs for jobs' sake, with not a great deal of interest in what the outcome of the system is, all paid for by hard-working people's hard-earned money paid in taxes.

Privatise something and the concept of wanting better customer outcomes to compete with competition is perfectly logical. Because without competition, there is nothing to stop the giddy drive for profit right now. Long-term investment is considered pretty pointless in many privatised companies, especially as it uses up profits which could be distributed to shareholders right now, keeping share prices good, and high and achieving excellent bonuses for those in charge.

In short, neither privatisation or state-ownership will ever be perfect – and once you accept that fact then you just work out which is the least bad option.

The Right to Buy scheme was followed by the total de-structuring of mortgage requirements, fuelling the new buy-to-let market. Soon the aspiration of 'owning your own home' became 'owning your own home plus a buy-to-let'. It doesn't take a mathematician to work out that this has a finite success level.

But for a homeowner the reality is that once you get to old age and have scraped and saved to pay off your mortgage, you're now likely to have to sell your home to pay for your care – a cynic could say this enforced carrot-style way of saving for just this might have always been the plan.

Insecurity of tenure in the UK is another driving force for the 'buyer' rather than 'renter' market.

Whether the government actively encouraged or incompetently failed to notice, there has been a massive increase in the private part-time incidental landlord be they for social housing or private rental housing. The trouble is there are just too many variables in private landlords lives to mean they are able to give security of tenure to a tenant in a property that they don't know if they can/will/want to own in six months, let alone six or twenty years.

All of which adds up to a broken rental market in the UK, which in turn fuels the desire to buy your own home. Don't get me wrong. I'm not saying DON'T buy; I'm just saying you don't or at least shouldn't HAVE to buy to be a complete human being.

In other countries it is quite normal to always rent and save money in other ways over your working life. It is normal, too, to invest emotionally and financially in your rental home, perhaps fitting a kitchen you love or redecorating – in the UK a combination of reasons means that renting is very often considered a short-term stopgap.

I believe we don't need more homes per se, we just need more *affordable* homes to buy or rent. Utterly key though is to invest in really great infrastructure to get people cheaply and quickly to and from the housing we already have around the country. We do have lots of houses that are affordable in the UK, it's just that they are in far less accessible places with fewer job opportunities.

Housing in the UK is a hot topic with so many variants, but I think it is fair to say despite all this that, yes, us Brits are obsessed with the concept of 'home'. A shelter for you and the people you love. Somewhere you can make special, surrounded by the things that make you feel secure and have meaning to you. Somewhere you can feel safe and come back to and that is a constant.

We humans are better in a community. We figured that out way back when we took shelter from the cold and the wet in caves. We learnt that being together made us happier and stronger than being alone – and where better to be together than under one roof where you can shut the door on the world outside?

Especially when that roof covers 40,000 square feet of house, with ninety-seven rooms and thirty-two bedrooms, and is absolutely magnificent.

A roof like the one at Rise Hall.

7

A crumbling stately home and a pair of stupidly romantic dreamers

Although my husband, children and work often try my patience and regularly make me question my sanity, I think in truth I have only ever really done one truly stupid thing in my life: buying Rise Hall.

What makes it worse is that I even knew it was a stupid decision at the time.

But then what is the point of a dream if you don't ever try and make it happen? There is nothing I like more than a challenge and from an early age I have always secretly reckoned that if you really believe something will happen, then it probably will.

I have also never been very good at being told no. In many ways, when somebody says no to me, I almost see it as a challenge of 'how' rather than what I suspect most people understand it to mean.

Risk is addictive and exciting – the one thing you can be sure of is that if you don't take any risks then nothing will happen. But if nothing happens then you need to be content with everything staying the same. I have often thought the worst that can happen is that you do take a risk and it doesn't work out. Then you just need the resilience to pick yourself up and work out another path – because there always is one, you just have to keep looking and keep walking forward.

Honestly though, I like an adventure and I like a risk. It has not always paid off but you either succeed or learn, and honestly I sometimes think learning can be more enjoyable in the long run than succeeding anyway – so in all scenarios it's a win-win.

As my father once said, just after Billy was born and I worried that I might not do a very good job of bringing him up: 'People benefit from adversity so if you do a terrible job he'll benefit from it but you probably won't – in which case he'll be fine anyway.'

Graham and I didn't initially set out to buy a state-ly home. It was just that in our quest to find unloved and unmodernised properties, or even just land with potential, we registered with all the property auction companies and received all the catalogues.

In those days they were delightfully glossy brochures that in themselves were coffee-table ready – which made me almost as good as the homes that had casually laid copies of *Homes & Gardens* and *Vogue* around (though in truth I think I just aspired to be that person but probably was more of a pile of 'stuff' person with various bits of junk mail still in its packaging, festering alongside unopened household bills!).

One day around twenty years ago, one particular lot in a brochure caught our eye. It was for a house called Revesby Abbey in Lincolnshire that looked not dissimilar to the Houses of Parliament, with a guide price of £55,000.

Even back then, £55,000 for a pile of house roughly the same size as Parliament, that would have cost probably £20 million to build, seemed a total bargain. Being just about within our financial reach, it was too impossibly tempting not to at least go and take a look at it.

And so our dream of owning and living in our very own stately home suddenly became a real-life possibility.

Revesby Abbey would once upon a time have been the showpiece entertainment home for the family that owned the several thousand acres surrounding it. It's these acres that would have provided the income required to employ the many dozens of staff needed to keep a building like this maintained.

The end of the nineteenth century and beginning of the twentieth century was a time of tremendous change. The First World War took its toll on the whole infrastructure of a stately home.

Then, during the Second World War, many homes like Revesby Abbey were forced to reduce down to a skeleton staff, with the men being called away to fight and the women having to take over many of their roles or focus on the war effort.

After this, things could never return to how they were

before, a tragedy for the English country house and the people that owned them, but perhaps rather fairer for the rest of the population!

The change was underpinned by economics: death duties reached the dizzy heights of 65 per cent during the Second World War. A demolished house was not able to be valued for probate duty though, so down they came. By 1955, country homes were being demolished at a rate of one every five days and several thousand in total.

Despite the Town and County Planning Act of 1944 enabling local authorities to protect these homes by listing them, there was little sentimental interest from either the public or local authorities to save them.

The updating of the Act in 1968 helped a little by making it compulsory to get permission to demolish a house rather than just 'inform' the local authority. However, it wasn't until after the highly publicised exhibition in 1974, 'The Destruction of the Country House 1875–1975', in the Victoria and Albert Museum, where a 'hall of destruction' showed illustrations of some of the demolished homes, that public opinion changed and the majority of architecturally and historically important homes started to be actively listed and protected.

And even if you did not demolish your house to save on death duties, most families simply could no longer afford to pay the dozens and dozens of staff that these houses needed to run.

Without staff, the houses were just unable to be kept in a good state of repair. In turn this meant they weren't much fun to live in. So families began to move out.

However, even though they had abandoned the house, the families tended not to move very far because they often still wanted to live on and farm the land – it being the major asset and producing income.

This meant moving into one of the smaller homes on the estate, or sometimes a house that had been built for the widow of a previous owner of the estate upon her husband dying and son taking over. Sometimes they took over the vicarage where the vicar had previously been housed, sometimes to a lodge for an estate manager that was pimped up to be a bit more appropriate for this relative 'downsize'. Sometimes the families built new houses or they bought a nearby village manor house.

Then, knowing they would never want the money pit of the main house again, but now being unable to demolish it, but still with the hefty price tag of maintenance, the owners often tried to get rid of them. The trouble was they often didn't really want to sell the houses as they were generally built in the middle of their land and, perhaps understandably, they didn't really want somebody else owning a lump of land and property often slap-bang in the middle of their estate.

Especially as by then, the cost of maintaining let alone running those houses meant that they would sell for almost nothing.

Some enlightened owners found alternative solutions such as opening them up to the public and diversifying into tourism, such as Longleat. Others opened up hotels or schools or divided them into flats or vertically split apartments. Some were rented to local authorities for offices.

So, in this respect, the 'Grade Listing' worked. As frustrating as it was for the landowners who often would rather turn the footprint of where a stately home stood back to productive farmland, I do personally think that when so many of the earth's resources had been used to create these massive spectacular buildings, it does seem wrong to demolish them just because they didn't have a purpose for society at that nanosecond in time.

Thankfully, in my opinion, many of our more interesting buildings – be they factories or homes – were saved.

And not only could owners no longer simply demolish them, but also the owner now had a legal obligation to repair and maintain them.

If they didn't then the local authority was – and still is – entitled to carry out essential repairs to stabilise the building and the cost of these repairs can be claimed back through court from the registered owner or assets seized to that value and sold.

Nature doesn't take long to reclaim a building if it is not constantly maintained. If the gutters aren't cleared of leaves the rain gets in, and once the rain gets in the rot sets in, and before you know it, large sections of the building are literally falling down.

***

Roll forward fifty-odd years to around 1990 and we found ourselves standing outside Revesby Abbey. We had to abandon the car, walk across a farm, then wade through waist-high undergrowth that would have, once upon a time, been manicured lawns.

The complicated story of the house itself unfurled. Despite it being listed, the lead gutterwork had been removed, possibly stolen for scrap but a sure-fire way to let water in and let nature take over.

The water had indeed got in and large sections of the house had rampaging dry rot. Dry rot is like a mushroom that simply loves nice moist, dark, undisturbed homes to live in and eats the moisture out of the wet wood. The downside is that removing ALL the moisture from wet wood also removes its structural integrity, meaning that massive timbers that hold up roofs end up with cracks across the grain, turning the timber into little, tiny blocks and in some places just dust itself.

You can tell a bad outbreak of dry rot in a building such as this – it has a fine layer of ginger spores that look like dust across everything. These are the spores sent out from a fruiting body, which is the heart of the rot, looking for more suitable areas that are nice, damp and undisturbed to get their teeth stuck into and set up home.

It also spreads, sending out tentacles called hyphae and mycelium that look a bit like cobwebs that can travel behind plaster and through gaps in brickwork in search of more food. Dry rot is a bit like a cancer and indeed is often called the cancer of buildings. Wet rot at least remains localised in a section of wet wood. Once you remove the moisture it is unable to live as it is too weak to travel and look for pastures new.

Revesby Abbey was full of dry rot (and probably wet rot too). The cavernous entrance hall held a sweeping staircase, but the rot had caused the top section to collapse leaving the last remaining stair treads precariously jutting out of the wall. Meanwhile, above us, you could see blue sky peeping through the heavily ornate plasterwork on the ceiling.

The patterned floor, as we trailed across it, was covered in a layer of decaying leaves and organic debris that had presumably blown in over the years. We wandered through room after room of resplendent crumbling decoration, now a graveyard to the many birds and rodents that had taken it up as their home since the humans had left.

Much of the house couldn't be accessed as it was too dangerous, but we saw enough to be in wonderment of this unloved dinosaur of a bygone era.

Thankfully some semblance of sense came to us and we didn't buy Revesby Abbey, the combination of how far the rot had set in together with unresolved legal access issues and the title not having really any land around the house made it more than we wanted to take on. However the visit was a bit like starting a love affair. Our new obsession and passion became seeking out these 'buildings at risk'.

We spent the next ten years happily looking around these unwanted gargantuan relics of the past, dreaming of what they had once been and imagining the scenes that might have played out within their magnificent walls.

The more we found out, the more fascinating these buildings became to us. Sometimes they weren't technically for sale. Occasionally, they were even boarded up. But we learnt that if you waded through the overgrown gardens there was often an open door or window you could sneak in through.

There was always a moment in each house where, wandering around in awe and ignoring all the repercussions and sensible reasons why you shouldn't, we would consider the fact that it might actually be possible to afford to buy and then live in a stately home – albeit not as it once would have been like, being waited on hand and foot (or even without the rain coming in). But for a stupidly romantic couple of dreamers like us, it was always a pretty amazing fantasy meets reality moment.

8

Why you should never view a house on a beautiful day

Finally, when I was twenty-eight and Graham was twenty-seven, we came across a house called Rise Hall being advertised in the *Yorkshire Post*.

The house no longer owned its main drive but this, we had learnt, was not uncommon as the drive meandered across land that was rarely for sale *with* the house. So the gatehouses at the far end of the drive were also not included.

However, it did look beautiful.

So Diccon, Graham and I set off and a few hours later drove up the back drive in our slightly dented bright red Ford Sierra, which had definitely seen better days, pulling up in front of the stable block that would have once housed sixty-odd horses.

It was summer and it was intriguing.

WARNING: You should never view any home you are considering buying on a beautiful day. On a sunny day in the UK there is something so excruciatingly lovely about almost anywhere that you would be forgiven for parting with your hard-earned cash to literally end up living in a wheely bin.

As we wandered around the endless rooms and down the sweeping staircase, it all suddenly seemed possible.

The magnificent library was still intact (apart from one section of ceiling that would at some point need its decorative plasterwork to be repaired and presumably the leak above it), but we had repaired plasterwork in houses in London and knew what this entailed. Indeed all of the rooms at Rise had sections of damaged plasterwork from the rain getting in but more was intact than not!

The roof was largely intact and not leaking as much as many of the other country houses we had seen. (We'd seen one stately home where a previous owner had a boat-building company and fibre-glassed over all the slates to try and keep the water out, but some years later the roof had started to leak again. The fibreglass that had stuck forever to the slates rendered every single slate unable to be reused – it also meant that when it failed by cracking in random places, the rainwater ran through cracks in the fibreglass and along some distance before it got in, meaning tracing leaks would have been almost impossible.)

You couldn't see the sky through the roof and whilst it clearly had some dry rot, it wasn't rampaging through the rest of the building yet which appeared to still be largely structurally sound.

Rise Hall also owned the land around it, thirty acres in total, which, although a very long way from a farm that might carry with it the benefits of some form of income, seemed to us a good amount. (Clearly thirty acres is a MASSIVE amount of land to have with a cottage or in a city or village, but it's not when it's in the middle of nowhere with the building itself sitting on much of it.)

We had looked at one house where there was only one acre with the house and that was all at the front as a glorified driveway. The land to the back had been sold off for housing under planning guidance called 'enabling development'.

In this instance somehow permission had been given for houses to be built with gardens that quite literally went up in strips to the back of the house, meaning you looked out of half the windows and straight into people's back gardens. You couldn't even walk around the outside of the house at all. Even if you didn't mind the lack of privacy, the lack of access for maintenance would have been a nightmare.

Rise also still had its stable block with it, rather than it having been carved off and either developed or sold to someone else. In short, it owned everything around it and was private – we liked that.

Lastly, we worked out it was less than four hours' drive to London and was only one hour from York and Leeds, so wasn't nearly as isolated as some of the houses we'd looked at. We'd looked at one in the Outer Hebrides – which was hardly commuting distance back to London!

During the Second World War, Rise Hall had been used by the army. Afterwards, a convent took it over and opened up a girls' boarding school which it was for just over forty years. In our years there, we came across 'old girls' all over the country doing all sorts of different things and it was always a joy to make these connections. Amazingly, in a weird full-circle way, when we built our new house in Somerset, it turned out one of our decorators had been to school at Rise Hall.

Although the school had long been closed and the nuns long gone by the time we came along, many ex-pupils visited us, all of them looking brilliantly guilty as they walked down the main stairs, which were out of bounds when they had been there. We'd often sit halfway down the stairs and have a glass of wine with them in a final joyous act of school rebellion.

The family that had occupied Rise Hall before the Second World War had moved into the vicarage across the park. The vicarage overlooked the park, making it totally understandable that it wasn't for sale with the house, but Rise Hall enjoyed views over it too.

The park was designed by renowned horticulturalist and landscape architect Lancelot 'Capability' Brown. In the eighteenth century it had two wildlife-filled lakes, one of which even had its own island.

It also had beautifully planted specimen trees, one of

which was close enough to our boundary to negotiate a tiny extra piece of land to be included in the sale, which was crucial to me at the time because I had plans to attach a swinging bench to it and while away the hours as if I inhabited a Jane Austen novel.

Twenty-odd years later when we sold Rise Hall, I had not only still not fitted the swinging seat, but I can't imagine I would ever have had the time to sit on it anyway. (We did, I am pleased to say, have one in our home in London where we spent countless sunny afternoons with tiny children. It honestly was an oasis that delivered all you could wish for, especially with a glass of rosé as the evening drew in.)

The house was for sale for £375,000, which you have to consider in relative terms. It was a lot of money in some ways but far less than many of the three- or four-bedroom houses we were then developing and selling in not particularly smart parts of London. Rise Hall had stood empty for ten years whilst the family had tried to find a new use or owner for the building.

Graham and I, young and responsibility-free and having had a successful property development and rental business for ten years, decided that we would put all our personal money outside of the business, which we had thought we would use to buy a family home in London, into buying Rise Hall instead.

It went to sealed bids, we put in our offer of the asking price. Looking back, I'm not sure we were taken that seriously. I think the estate agent, who generally dealt with smarter and older customers, was not convinced that we had the grit/money/know-how/nerve/sheer bloody-minded determination to actually see the purchase through. I suspect the fact that we were in our twenties, wearing scruffy paint-splattered jeans and driving an old Ford Sierra didn't help.

Our bid was rejected.

We were gutted but also a bit surprised, as you cannot look at a 'building at risk' without adding on the cost of repairs and then subtracting it from an end value – and when you looked at it this way £375,000 was a lot of money to be asking. However, clearly there were other people who had plans for Rise Hall and had drilled down into the 'what to do with Rise Hall' question and had come up with something better than we had.

So instead, Graham and I decided to buy a family home together in London and began an extensive refurbishment project on it.

But then, quite literally three weeks after completing the purchase and starting work on the London house we got a phone call to say the other purchasers for Rise Hall had backed out. Did we still want it?

The answer was yes.

A frantic race was then on to finish the house in London, which at this stage was a gutted building site, and sell it in order to raise the money to buy Rise Hall.

It took about four months. In the meantime, we delayed

as long as possible and eventually had to exchange, negotiating a delayed completion in five months' time. The closer completion got without the house in London selling, the hairier it was and the more I wondered what on earth we had done. But as luck would have it, a buyer came along and, whilst we did go up to the wire of two weeks after the completion due date, we hit both our sale and our purchase at the last minute on the last day.

In fact, the deals were done as we were driving up the M1 in a couple of Luton vans loaded with our possessions, ready to move in. Rise Hall with its magnificent roof, 40,000 square feet, ninety-seven rooms, thirty-two bedrooms and thirty acres of land was a dream come true and somehow it was just meant to be.

9

Fish and chips and no running water

If you had asked us separately, both Graham and I would have given different reasons as to why we went ahead with buying Rise Hall.

I think I thought perhaps we'd have bucketfuls of babies and maybe, just maybe, the sepia version of my life, which was based a mix of *The Waltons*, *The Dukes of Hazzard* and a costume drama, might just somehow happen if we were to live inside this building of dreams.

Graham's vision was less based in reality than mine. He just didn't honestly think I'd go ahead with the purchase. As I've often said, when one person in a couple has dreams and the other makes things happen it's a very dangerous combination indeed.

I did once ask Graham with a smirk, 'If I buy you a stately home will you like me more?', which he skirted answering.

I still have the card he gave me in my drawer of sentimental missives from him and the children – it's a beautifully hand-drawn doodle on a folded-over scrap of paper and inside it says: 'Thank you for buying me a stately home last week.'

In the end, it wasn't so much that we had decided to buy Rise Hall but more that the reasons not to buy it were running out. And then a friend said, 'You should stop talking about these silly stately homes – you're never going to actually buy one.'

And I think that was the deciding moment. As I mentioned earlier, I don't like being told I can't do something – it's almost like a dare to me.

So there it was – we were heading up the motorway in two hired Luton vans stuffed full of items we had spent the last ten years collecting and storing.

We had the unwanted contents from my family home with our mother, the unwanted contents from my grand-parents' home of fifty years, the unwanted contents of Graham's grandparents' home of fifty years and the un-wanted contents of Graham's parents' home of twenty years.

The combined decades of multiple generational posses-sions doesn't even bear thinking about. Not to mention the unwanted contents of various houses we had bought to develop that hadn't been cleared out and had furniture that was considered rubbish left in them (which we had sanded, repainted, repolished and generally repaired).

A great friend who had been working at a hotel in London designing their lighting had been told all the beds were being replaced and, knowing of our adventure, asked them if rather than them having to pay to clear the old ones, they would like us to remove them. So we had thirty not-too-badly stained and very good-quality beds travelling up with us too.

When we bought Rise Hall it didn't even have running water, as whilst empty its ancient external underground pipework had finally perished and so it had been disconnected some years before.

However, there were still several school bathrooms with endless rows of baths and showers and basins albeit with no actual running water to fill them.

We had asked the estate manager if he would be kind enough to oversee getting a new water supply put in, which was done between exchange and completion in our absence so we would have cold water when we moved in. But very quickly we had hot water too as Diccon and Graham had spent the week before in our office in London collecting all the parts and, like a giant set of Meccano, building a 'portable plug-in' hot water system, which was effectively a hot water cylinder with expansion tank and immersions all fitted together, which we could put into a room next to one of the many bathrooms.

They'd assembled it and we then lifted the entire system onto the roof of one of the Luton vans, complete with valves and controls attached, and strapped it down. This piece of cunning genius meant that we were able to lift the pre-built entire system off the Luton van and carry it complete upstairs. Then we just screwed a board with taps already fitted onto the wall above one of the baths with the tails of hot and cold pipes connected. These tails were pushed through a couple of holes we drilled through the wall and connected to the hot water cylinder system in the next-door room, which was in turn plugged into the wall. In short, two holes drilled, two screws into the wall, two push fit connectors – and twenty minutes later we had hot running water in one of the baths. A hot bath when there is zero chance of heating apart from an open fire is very welcome indeed in the winter.

As for a kitchen, we had a very decrepit old standalone four-ring electric cooker my grandmother had had in her shed. We put it in a room at the front of the house, which we decided would be a good place for a kitchen – and would indeed become our kitchen for the next couple of decades.

There was some debate on this as kitchens in stately homes always evolved to be right at the back of a house like this where the staff would be. However, now we spend so much of our time in a kitchen, it seemed absurd to have the best rooms at the front of the house standing empty whilst we hung out all day right at the back near the bins. Sometimes you have to be bold making an old house work for modern living. As the room had been used for science lessons it had a slightly chipped sink in the corner – but a sink is a sink!

Very excitingly we also discovered some old free standing 1970s melamine kitchen units in one of these dingy old rooms at the back of the house where the nuns had their kitchen, and we dragged them to the front room too. A perfect makeshift kitchen.

Not bad for our first day.

All that was left to do was to put a mattress on the floor of the room we chose to be our bedroom – by this point we didn't even have time to dust off the thin layer of flies across the floorboards.

Then, on their very kind insistence, we headed to our neighbours' house for supper. It was these neighbours, Hugh and Booey, who had sold us Rise Hall. We arrived and both they and the estate manager, Andrew, and his wife, Carol, were there too in the kitchen, laughing and drinking wine together. We couldn't have felt more welcome and more at home and, walking back to Rise Hall across the park at 3 a.m. having had the most delicious shepherd's pie, we knew we had made four new lifelong firm friends.

After they invited us over on our first night at Rise Hall, we returned the invitation. Our rudimentary kitchen meant we had to make do with bags of salad and cold meat, cheese and bread, but the wine flowed and the company was most excellent.

Our neighbours were brilliantly hospitable. If you turned up at 6 p.m. you were always offered a glass of wine; then, if you didn't leave for home by 8 p.m., you'd be offered supper, which was always eagerly accepted. Both couples included us in their lives and introduced us to their friends and families, many of whom we are still really close to. We couldn't have been luckier.

Hugh and Booey had three joyous sons, who were about eight to twelve when we met them, and we watched them grow into utterly joyous men, now all married with babies of their own. When our third son, Raffey, arrived, we made their third son, Nick, his godfather. Nick now lives near us in Bristol and has a really excellent restaurant called Snobby's. He and his lovely wife, Alice, have just had their first son and have asked Raffey to be Rudy's godfather, which Raffey is utterly thrilled about and so the friendship is now thoroughly cemented down generations.

But that was all still to come.

Back then, and on our second night, Diccon, Caroline and our two much-adored nephews, Theo and Orlando, arrived with some other friends to help christen the house.

It was a bitterly cold January night. We sat in the library surrounded by all the chairs that came with us and boxes piled up everywhere, eating fish and chips. I learnt the valuable lesson the hard way that the fat on the chip paper puts a fire out rather than making it go up in flames, which made me very unpopular!

This was also in the days before we owned a genius electric Grenadier fire lighter that every home with any kind of fire should own.

We shivered and laughed and toasted the beginning of our crazy but thrilling new adventure.

10

Christmas at Rise Hall

It was January 2001 and we set ourselves the target of getting the house civilized enough by the following Christmas to host our large extended family – all forty-nine of us.

It was a good goal to have, and an excellent incentive to get things done.

First up we converted one section of the house into a kitchen, sitting room and bedrooms for Diccon, Caroline and their young family to use so they had their own independence whilst they were there. We had the same at the other end of the house.

In the evenings that followed we'd invite each other 'over to supper'. This involved walking down the North corridor and knocking on each other's kitchen doors to invite them. The invitation was occasionally declined, which was fine, but more often than not it wasn't, which meant that Asda's trusty Big Red Wine Box would be pulled out and consumed under the guise of keeping us warm.

We scrubbed the rooms of their black mould, then some very boring but very affordable large tubs of gardenia-coloured paint were liberally dispersed around the walls of the house by us and our very lovely decorator, Karen, who ended up working with us for years.

I actually met Karen on the first series of the TV show I had started to present by then. We were filming a barn conversion in Lincolnshire and she was working for a really inspiring couple called Philip and Stephen. Meeting them would set off one of the hundreds of weird, serendipitous chains of events that have happened in my life.

I'd started chatting to Karen, who was working on their barn, and it turned out she had travelled down to Lincolnshire from much nearer Rise Hall and, knowing literally no one in East Yorkshire, I grabbed her number.

Philip and Stephen were utterly lovely too. I decided to swap numbers and invited them to come and stay in our largely derelict stately home. They came – then invited us back to stay with them and we became firm friends.

In fact, it was the catering company called Dine, who we were so impressed with when we went to Philip and Stephen's wedding, that, when later down the line we decided to do weddings at Rise Hall, were the obvious people to contact and ask if they would like to get involved.

It was then the owners of Dine, Dan and Helen Gill, who eventually, nineteen years later, ended up buying

Rise Hall. I often think what a weird small world of coincidences it is but in fact you can trace back so much of what has happened in our lives to taking a bit of a leap of faith. Opportunities in life spring out of action and activity, and positive things seem to happen when you make positive choices.

Anyway, back to the leap of faith that was Rise Hall.

Our biggest problem was that there were leaks in most of the rooms – which was ironic because, actually, one of the most magnificent things about Rise was its roof. It had a large, flat leaded section in the middle you could walk on, with two large roof lanterns that stuck up like a couple of greenhouses.

There were twenty-six chimneys, many of which had had their chimney pots removed and had been capped off over the years, presumably to keep the draft out but also as it would have been cheaper than repointing and restoring each one.

Running around the edge of the main roof in a square was a pitched roof. You could run up the lead valleys to the ridge. Standing there, surveying the world below, the view was utterly spectacular. You really could be-lieve you were on top of the world. A careful walk along the ridge would get you to a valley descending down the other side, where there was another lead gutter that ran around the inside of a foot-high parapet running the whole way around the house.

Inside the outer slopes was a maze of internal roof

73

spaces, some of which were more accessible than others and some with absurdly designed internal open trough gutters that carried the rainwater from the central flat roof section to behind the outer parapet.

These, and every other water-carrying gulley, hopper and hole, were inhabited by rooks' nests with literally thousands of carefully collected twigs. These mini-dams ensured that instead of the rainwater flowing through these fairly stupidly designed gutters in the first place, it would flow over the top and down into the bed-room below.

Every time it rained a call went out and anyone and everyone would grab a raincoat and handful of buck-ets and run up to the bedrooms and roof space to see whether previous repairs had worked and where new ones were required.

Dozens and dozens of sacks of twigs and debris later the labyrinth of water runs were clear. Then we used various gluey products to splodge over the cracks in the lead. Lead is a brilliant product but once it has had its shelf life – about 150 years – it really has to be replaced.

The trouble is the lead is the first layer to go down on a roof, so replacing it properly requires you to strip off the slates and start again. We couldn't afford this at the time and were certainly not going to go into debt doing it, as we knew the whole project of Rise didn't make financial sense anyway, so we kept up with the gunge and buckets.

Our endless plugging of the roof seemed to work and we were excitedly working towards our epic Christmas.

By December we'd made huge progress. The front section of the house was largely habitable-ish. All the beds had electric blankets (which we'd go round turning on at about 6 p.m. every night when people were staying).

Bedside tables, most of which were upturned boxes with pieces of fabric over them, were put in place. All the rooms had a large bottle of water and glasses and a couple of sachets of Resolve, the partied-too-hard-last-night next-morning medicine (necessary after the Big Red Wine Box!).

Admittedly there was still only one working bathroom, which had to be shared by all thirty-two bedrooms, but we had at least taken out the dividing melamine cubicles and all but one bath, basin and loo so it no longer felt so much like a school bathroom.

With just one loo, one shower, one bath and one basin in it, the room was now enormous, so we put an old armchair in there in case anyone wanted someone to keep them company whist they were in the bath.

Then, just as we were wondering where to go and buy a Christmas tree, the estate tractor arrived towing the farm trailer carrying a huge one. It had been sent by our very lovely neighbours Hugh and Booey.

It only *just* fitted into the library and from then on, Christmas always started with the magical gift of a tree arriving from our new friends to the squeals of delight from the ever-growing number of children (and adults if I'm honest) who kept arriving at Rise Hall for Christmas.

That first year, Hugh and Booey also sent their lovely gamekeeper, John Naylor, whom I became really fond of, round with a 'brace of pheasants' – a brace is a pair for those of you who don't come from the country. They were dead but still with feathers on and tied together with a bit of baler twine at the neck.

I'd seen braces of pheasant at people's houses when I was a child, but my father didn't shoot apart from when we were short of meat and money, and even then it tended to be a small rabbit that went in a stew without me joining the dots.

So I did know of people who lived around us who went shooting, but it was the first time I'd personally been given a pair of pheasants as a present and it was a custom I was unfamiliar with. I was super grateful and took them in – and immediately asked Graham to deal with them.

Stupidly, I then later admitted my lack of experience to either Hugh or Booey, and the following Christmas John delivered a bag of diced pheasant breast – without a barcode but not far short – but with a wry smile for which I liked him even more!

That very first Christmas was chaotic but glorious.

We had our electric four-ringed cooker, but it was so far from the old fuse board and the ring main wasn't powerful enough so when we plugged it in, it tripped the electrics.

Thankfully our great friend the electrical designer (the same friend who blagged us the second-hand beds!) rigged up a cable through the hole in the ceiling where the light fitting went and connected it into the upstairs ring main, which had far less demand on it.

We also invested in a thoroughly brilliant plug-in electric steamer and a microwave, and between all that we cooked a pretty amazing Christmas lunch – even if the enormous turkey had to be pushed into the tiny oven with the bottom of my foot.

That first year we started new traditions such as 'bring one and only one Christmas decoration each', meaning we now have the BEST eclectic collection of decorations from all over the world.

We have peacocks made of feathers, bizarre shiny fairies and Father Christmas in all sorts of guises made from all sorts of different materials. We have children's creations signed by their fair hands that make me smile every year I lift them carefully out of their box.

We played plenty of games, drank way too much, stayed up too late, ate too many chocolates and made memories with the massive extended family I am so lucky and privileged to have.

Weekends at Rise were always filled with fun and laughter. Friends would often jump on a train on a Friday night and stay until Sunday. There was generally a 'project' and everyone would get stuck in for a few hours before someone would open a bottle of wine or two.

It was a true party house and honestly – whilst it was a LOT of hard work – the pleasure was certainly worth every inch of pain. I look back on that time now with such happiness, not only was I living the domestic dream in this stately home but my career in television was just about to begin.

11

Our wonderful Rise Hall wedding

About a year or so after we bought Rise Hall, Graham asked me to marry him – largely because I had suggested that if he wasn't going to ask me, I would get pregnant instead and I think he thought he could stave that one off with a proposal.

I had learnt by that time in my life in a negotiation you should never make a threat you weren't going to see through, and I was quite happy with both those options. The 'splitting up or marriage' option could have gone horribly wrong as I was looking for confirmation of commitment *not* to be single.

We were busy painting windows at the time, when he asked me to come to the roof to look at something. Off I went and followed him as he climbed up one of the valleys to the ridge and we sat down. Then, as we perched on the ridge of our mad and stupid folly of a house with the sun going down, looking over the beautiful Capability Brown parkland, Graham finally, after ten years of living together, popped the question.

It's the only time I have ever seen him tongue-tied. I thought about saying no for a second but figured he'd probably dump me if I did, which I definitely didn't want, plus he had a really big sapphire ring that I very much wanted to model, so I said yes. So far so good – we are now thirty years into living together and twenty years into marriage.

Getting married seemed really quite a commitment but actually I think buying Rise Hall was a bigger one – as was having children. I often think a marriage is so, so much easier to get out of than all the other things you end up sharing when you are with someone – so much so that the actual marriage itself becomes rather incidental in many ways.

Nevertheless, I don't plan on ever marrying again so it was a big deal.

We went round and round in circles trying to decide whether to have a big or small wedding. We had a moment where we thought we might just drive to Gretna Green Registry Office in our jeans one afternoon.

But I knew for my father, a church warden for most of his adult life and who had great faith, a non-church wedding was something he'd eventually get over but would much rather not have to. So, bearing in mind we didn't much care and I am a fan of the cultural, social and historical upsides of Christianity and indeed most religions, we figured we might as well have our wedding in a church.

We decided we'd have a massive party at home in Rise Hall to celebrate and so handed the actual wedding over to my father and stepmother. It was in their local church near Chichester.

Although everyone talks about how stressful weddings can be, ours turned out to be such a chilled day. Graham and I woke in our little flat in London where we stayed when we had to be in town for work.

We drove down to Chichester and then my brother took Graham to the church via the pub for a quick drink whilst my father drove me there in his bullnose Morris classic car. Trying to make light of the slightly tense atmosphere on the short drive, I quipped, 'Well if it doesn't work out we can always get divorced.' My father didn't respond, which was disappointing as I thought I was being rather funny!

The church seated about two hundred people – but there were only about twenty of us. We had our parents and siblings – although with all my step-siblings that's quite a lot, especially when you include their accompanying families and my assorted cousins.

We did think about also inviting a friend or two but couldn't work out who to invite so ended up not inviting any.

As for music, we decided to take a tape recorder and sing a hymn as everyone coming loved singing and to be honest music has always been a very big part of both our lives. 'Jerusalem' won as we all liked it most.

We then all went back to my father and stepmother's house for coronation chicken, and Graham and I left shortly after for a night at a lovely hotel called The Clifton.

A month later, in October 2002, we had our wedding reception for 200 guests in the 1970s sports hall at Rise, which actually leaked more than the 1870s house itself. We spent ages beforehand mopping the floor! We pinned an awful lot of dust sheets down the walls to mask the green mould that covered them, then we carefully lit them with spotlights to make it look a bit 'arty'.

I think we have always been a bit miserly – or maybe it's just what I perceive as money being wasted (or perhaps we just didn't have the money to spare). Either way, we didn't have a florist, instead we got a load of tealights from Ikea and we picked some greenery from the garden that we stuck on the tables.

I often think that if we were to decorate from the garden now we could do it *so* much better, as almost everything in nature is beautiful if you display it in the right way – plus I have a gorgeous friend Pip now who also loves all things natural and sees beauty in it all, and if I roped her in we could make it quite magnificent. Youth is terribly wasted on the young.

We didn't have a cake but instead had a big pile of chocolate brownies made by an old friend. We had dinner, speeches and dancing, and, as always with Rise, it turned into a brilliant, if a little chaotic, party that went on all night with dozens of friends staying in the rooms upstairs.

There was a hierarchy when the house was full where the better-decorated bedrooms nearer the only bathroom were given to the more important people and the thirty-second bedroom, which was still full of mould and flies and had a hole in the floor (though still with a very comfy bed in it), to less important people.

The system went along the lines of need, so anyone ill, pregnant or with a small baby was much higher up the list – newly met or newly engaged was next up there, then right at the bottom of the importance list, just below single teenage girls, were single teenage boys (who didn't seem to ever care where they slept). But wherever anybody slept, at least they were guaranteed a comfortable bed.

Being a terrible bed snob, the rooms may not have been redecorated for years but they did have very comfortable sheets with thick mattress covers, electric blankets (in the years before we had heating) feather duvets and many, many feather pillows (which are actually much cheaper than you think they would be).

When we owned Rise Hall, people came and stayed – a lot. This was partly because it was right on the east coast near Hull and so not obviously 'on the way' to anywhere, so when people made the trip to see us, they'd generally stay at least one night. I also think this was because of how comfortable I made sure our beds were.

The post-wedding parties at Rise continued for another year or so until I got pregnant and had our first son, Billy. It was at this point we had to make a decision. We realised we could no longer be fluid and flexible with where we were living.

12

A new home and the mother of all goodbye parties

By this time, Diccon and Caroline were settled in London with three children now, two of whom had started school.

My TV work didn't appear to be the one-second wonder I had expected it to be and the channel seemed to want more. Not being one to turn things down, I thought I'd keep going down this route (and anyway I enjoyed it), but it was largely based around London.

Meanwhile Graham had decided to focus fairly full-time on painting. His studio was in Rise Hall but as an artist he could have been based anywhere. With nursery school looming so too would come term times and weekly commitments; a whole new world we had left behind many years before. So we decided to leave our nomadic lives behind and move full-time back to the tiny flat above our office in south London.

We then ended up with a really bizarre MASSIVE weekend holiday home in the form of Rise Hall, which whilst fun, didn't really make sense. So we had the even bigger decision of what we were going to do with Rise Hall if we weren't going to use it all the time.

So we decided to let it out as a wedding venue with a view to making it earn its keep whilst it was sitting empty. This also gave us a reason to fully restore the house and we set about a major refurbishment.

I believe that whilst you can have many houses you can only have one home. When we decided our home was in London and we would be renting Rise Hall out, it was only a matter of time, as is always the case with shifting sands, that other things would soon change.

As Billy got bigger, I realised our flat in London, which had been perfect for Graham and I when it was just the two of us, was not going to work long term. We hoped to have at least one sibling for Billy (secretly I was planning five but didn't like to admit it to Graham!), so we started looking for a family home in London. Having developed lots of houses I was keen to buy somewhere that was a bit unusual.

There is a formula to a terraced house. They come in pretty standard layouts and rarely have much variation once you get to know them. By now we had developed so many that I knew them and their nuances inside out, and I wanted to live in a house that when you walked down the pavement you wouldn't be able to predict what the layout would be inside.

Admittedly, I had seen a few pretty radical changes,

such as putting the kitchen in the front room or upstairs, but because people are generally fairly similar and they have their set ways of living, trying to suggest they live in a totally non-ergonomic way is never going to really work.

So the hunt was on for a site, or a disused factory, or something, anything, that would be exciting and, I guess, challenging. Then, just before Billy's first birthday we found it.

Just outside Balham in south London, we found a third of an acre that housed an old gardener's cottage from a large country house that had been demolished around the turn of the twentieth century. A large lump of Streatham had been built in its place and on its land.

There was an old driveway that ran between two houses down to the end of their gardens, where there was a pair of wooden gates and a little wooden door; through this door was a path with overhanging trees that led around another house.

Finally, you emerged into the most beautiful garden, which had been carefully manicured and planted over the last twenty years by a super keen and highly skilled passion gardener. The house itself was nestled in a far corner of the garden but before we even got to the front door, we both whispered to each other, 'Let's buy this.'

We offered the asking price on the condition we could exchange and complete in the next three weeks – I was really keen to secure it and it was Billy's first birthday then, so it seemed like a good deadline and anyway the vendors were desperately keen to sell.

Three weeks later we moved in and celebrated Billy's birthday in the garden the next day with family and friends. I'd love to pretend he was fully engaged in the event but I think we can all be honest when we say that first birthday parties for our children are all about us – we choose a cake we like, invite the people we like and our child just sits on a hip. It was really just another excuse for a get-together with my brother and his family and great friends.

However, I told anyone who would listen that we'd bought the house as a birthday present for Billy – although once Billy's brothers started arriving I decided to not say this anymore for fear they all might one day actually take me seriously.

Before I knew it we had four sons and, although based in London, we still bundled our ever-increasing brood into the car or across London to King's Cross on the Tube, travelling up on the train to Rise Hall whenever we could.

The boys loved it there – all children loved it there. They would find something on wheels – roller blades, tricycles, skateboards – to go around the house as there was a perfect internal circuit of halls and corridors.

As more babies arrived they were pushed around by older siblings and friends. Faster and faster they would ride, making a hazard of walking in the opposite direction. A whole generation of children spent most of their holidays at Rise Hall. There was something magical about finding little pockets of children sitting on one of the many staircases or behind a door somewhere, locked in some imaginary world.

There were lots of made-up games, but especially popular were sardines and 'toilet tag'. This is a brilliant game introduced to us by my lovely late dear friend Maria. It's effectively tag, but when touched you have to assume a slightly crouched position with one arm out and someone has to sit down on you and push your arm down to flush to release you.

We had long walks to explore the area, often in search of a great pub with good food at the end. More children arrived – on one occasion fourteen adults walked the old railway line to Hornsea with six babies all stuffed in one old Silver Cross pram whilst countless other children trailed behind on bikes. Instead that day we had fish and chips there whilst sitting on the beach.

We had 'children's performances', which involved lining up chairs in the hallway and the adults buying carefully hand-crafted tickets from one of the children. Then one after another the children would dance, sing, play an instrument or even say a poem on the stage, which was generally on the stairs.

These performances were usually held after a considerable amount of Big Red Wine Boxes had been consumed at lunch or dinner, and there was always riotous applause and praise regardless of the quality or length of the performance, with the odd adult jumping up to perform too. Years later, my husband and sons have a pinch-yourself successful rock band – I do wonder whether this is where it all started from.

We had Easter, Christmas and new year housefuls and often Bonfire Night and a few birthdays too for good measure.

One New Year's Eve I remember particularly well.

We had by then 'rebranded' the old 1970s school sports hall into a ballroom for wedding guests, still good for football but kinder for rolling around and better for acoustics as it now had a carpet but football and chandeliers didn't see eye to eye. It was an excellent party venue though. We invited about a hundred and fifty adults who brought about eighty children ranging from one month to thirteen years old with them, and I thought I had come up with the perfect plan for enter-taining them all.

We collected all the rubbish accumulated over the festive period, all the boxes and containers, and put it in a massive pile in the morning room, which was one of the reception rooms.

My genius idea was to keep the children occupied by challenging them to take the rubbish and several rolls of tape and build it into a massive structure of some sort. It certainly kept them all quiet whilst all the adults had dinner and I went to bed feeling very pleased with myself.

The next morning with a fairly thick head, I woke to one of my children loudly whispering: 'Mummy, we've made snow!' Blurry-eyed, I went downstairs to find that I hadn't taken the white polystyrene packing pieces out of any of the boxes and the children had worked out that if they scraped them they could separate the little white balls which, then being static, had not only covered the whole room floor to ceiling but most of the corridors, and nearby rooms too!

The vacuum cleaner was going for the rest of the weekend with one person or another driving it but still even ten years later you'd find the odd tiny, little white surprise somewhere you weren't expecting it.

Rise was a rare and very special place for adults and children – you had space to see people and space to get away. It was massively informal, even once it was all refurbished and being rented out for weddings.

There was a joy to the fact that people generally came and stayed for a couple of nights and at some point whilst they were there, you'd actually get a chance to properly catch up, whereas when you met in the pub for a drink sometimes you never really got to have that conversation.

But Rise was becoming more and more successful as a wedding venue and as customers flooded in, so we reversed out of what had been our hugely happy home.

I felt increasingly embedded in London. What I also hadn't realised is that once children start school, whilst they are only there during the week during the term, they make friends that they want to see at the weekends and in the holidays.

This is when the birthday parties are, this is when the football clubs are, this is when their parents invite you over for Sunday lunch or supper on a Saturday night. This is also where you all meet up on the common and have a picnic and make lifelong friends. Not only the children, which they did, but also us parents too.

Being transient between two places had so many more disadvantages than I had anticipated, and they became clearer and clearer as the children got older.

I also slightly struggled with 'sharing' Rise Hall. I could never quite get my head around renting out our home with all our things in it. The more it became a venue, the less of our things were in it, and the cleaner and tidier and less homely it became.

It is also very, very hard to run a hospitality business when you are not actually there, and our commitments in London were coming thick and fast. Finding managers who shared a vision with you and wanted to implement plans in a consistent way was very tricky indeed.

In short, I think we needed to be there in person to really allow Rise Hall to fulfil its potential and being there just wasn't possible with everything else that was going on in our lives and the time it took to get there.

I think managing remotely is a challenge that takes a genius manager to handle and Graham and I may be many things but genius remote managers we are not.

When we finally did sell Rise Hall years later shortly after moving 'home' from London to Somerset, we had the most magnificent 'goodbye Rise Hall' party.

The generation of children who had spent most of their holidays at Rise Hall were all there for one last time – grown-up to a greater or lesser degree. They all remembered the 'one meal a day' weekends where they lined up for spag bol like a much nicer version of Oliver Twist.

In total we had around 200 friends and family – people who at one time or another had shared our Rise Hall adventure with us; the people who had made every penny and every moment of blood, sweat and tears worthwhile.

We once even managed to successfully matchmake a couple who we sat next to each other at my fortieth birthday party. He went to school with Graham and she was the youngest daughter of some great friends locally, but as they were the only people without children we thought it might be more fun for both of them to not have to do 'child talk'.

Talk they did – six months later they were married!

Now they have two children of their own and lived a few miles away from us in Somerset until moving back to Yorkshire last year. Life has its weird way of winding its tentacles around everything and creating a permanency that stretches beyond the walls of a building.

So when I say buying Rise Hall was a mistake, what I really mean is we could have done things that were more sensible with our money. But then Graham and I have never really 'done' sensible and there isn't one moment in one day that I have regretted our twenty-odd years in the East Riding and the memories we made there.

When we finally closed the door at Rise for the last time, I wasn't sad because we had already started our new adventure in Somerset. Had we not had that, I think it would have been a very different story. As it was, I just felt excited about the next experience.

The time had come for pastures new.

Property Ladder

A couple of months after we bought Rise Hall, I had a call out of the blue from a production company asking me to meet them. They wanted to discuss me working on a new show they were making called *Property Ladder*.

They said they were looking for contributors and a front face. I wasn't quite sure what either of these things were but went to meet the producers and did what they call a screen test – someone with a video camera recording me talking about the staff kitchen in the office.

After that I went to a coffee shop with the series producer, who later became a great friend, and we chatted through the premise of the show and, somewhat cheekily, I gave them some rather opinionated 'advice' on how I thought it should be made. Knowing quite literally *nothing* about making television and not even having watched *Grand Designs* at the time, which was the blueprint for this new series, I probably wasn't that helpful.

To my great surprise they phoned me a couple of days later and offered me the role of presenter. At the time we had a property investment company as well as a development company. Our businesses were doing really well and we had a really good quality of life and whilst I had dreamt of being a Hollywood actress I wasn't sure I particularly wanted to present television.

The channel wanted six episodes and each episode, they told me, would involve about twelve days of filming. To me – bearing in mind I had a stately home to renovate in time for Christmas! – seventy-two days filming was a very considerable amount of time.

I asked them what they were offering to pay. It was a pretty low fee – which for twelve days filming per show really wasn't that appealing. I said I'd think about it. They phoned back an hour later and doubled their offer, which was still not particularly enticing, given the age I was and the job I already had. I turned them down as it was less than I had been earning back in the Little Chef.

Then I had a long chat with my stepmother Boo who gave me one of her wise and sanguine pieces of advice. 'You only regret the things you don't do, not things you do.' She suggested I should do this series and then if I didn't enjoy it, I could always just turn down anything else.

To this day I often wonder where my life would have been if I had not taken her advice or she had not given it. It might have been better, it might have been worse, but I am sure of one thing – it definitely wouldn't have been as diverse.

I have met people I would never ever have otherwise met and learnt about things I would never have even known existed.

Over the years I have chatted to the leading experts on everything from bed bugs to fire safety, I've worked with the WWF, the Palace, the Royal National Lifeboat Institute, Royal Institute of Architects and the Building Research Institute to name a few.

I've learnt about the history, advantages and disadvantages of concrete, timber, steel, lime, slate, clay and straw as building materials.

I have met people with life stories that are so fascinating I don't even know where to start. And somehow, twenty years later, despite year on year assuming each series would probably be the last and I'd just get back to my day job, I still seem to be doing interesting projects for TV, meeting new and utterly brilliant individuals and learning new things about people I wouldn't have otherwise met. But filming that first episode, I had no idea of what was to come.

I look back now and think that if I'd watched the shows I was in for all those years, I probably could have been a much better presenter. However, for one reason or another I didn't, and I think there was an element of not-knowing that made it easier to compartmentalise my job from everyday life quite easily. I just carried on seeing the friends and family I had before, and I and everyone else really treated it just like I had changed jobs. Now in later life I am much more interested in the construction and production of a television documentary or show, but even then I had years of adult life behind me to keep me insulated from some of the less enjoyable elements of being in the public eye.

In fact, I think I am really lucky that TV came to me in my late twenties when even by then I already had a business, I had already met Graham and I had a large group of friends. Otherwise, I think you could get sucked up into the all-consuming world of the media if you weren't careful and start believing your own hype!

Life went on in the background. Graham and I got married and I fell pregnant with Billy. At the time we were filming a series of sixteen episodes of *Property Ladder* and, in order to get as much time off as possible after I had him, we filmed all the shows up to when Billy was born. This happened three more times with my other pregnancies – and so there are sixty-four episodes of *Property Ladder* where I go from not being pregnant to very pregnant indeed. This is why it sort of looks like I had sixty-four children!

Although I didn't really realise it at the time, in the early noughties there was still definitely a slight phobia about being pregnant and in the public eye, so being a working mother and carrying on normally whilst being pregnant and indeed turning up with a new-born baby to various board meetings and conferences in my normal work after giving birth was weirdly considered a pretty radical thing to do.

The truth is I genuinely wasn't making any political point at the time, I was just doing what I needed to do and just so happened to be pregnant. Attitudes have changed though and I am incredibly proud of any tiny part I had in making that happen as it's very weird indeed to me that something so utterly natural would be considered anything other than completely normal.

The mother 'juggle struggle' is one you just manage as you go along. I have made choices along the way, such as generally refusing to be away from home overnight, refusing filming abroad unless the children could accompany me and turning down events and dinners in place of being at home.

I would leave for filming at ungodly early hours and work through lunch in order to be back home in time for the kids' tea. We had loyal crew as they too were able to get home much earlier than they would normally have been able to. I was lucky though as I know in most jobs you wouldn't have been able to call the shots as I did. Somehow or another I genuinely feel I managed to be almost a full-time mother and simultaneously work full-time too.

13

Lots of noise, lots of animals and lots of children

Some thoughts on having children

From our second day at Rise, when Diccon and Caroline arrived with their two delicious small children in tow, I can't remember it ever not having little people around.

Babies in prams or being passed around in arms, crawling infants, toddlers climbing up things they shouldn't be climbing up (like Christmas trees) and small children charging around on some form of wheels or often being pushed by a cousin or sibling. Teenagers too, all making the most of the freedom Rise Hall gifted to us all.

But much as I loved all these children, no one can really tell you how much you'll love your child. I can't believe I actually worried about that before Billy arrived. I worried that a baby would be a bit like a guest that just won't leave and you slightly wish they'd go away.

I was also concerned that he might interfere with the

really lovely life and relationship Graham and I had. I was wrong though.

Although it wasn't like a thunderbolt of love when I first saw Billy – it was more a feeling of possession and anxiety. I knew he was mine and that felt good, but the responsibility, guilt and fear for him that arrived at the same time was terrifying.

I was worried I wasn't capable – I had an overwhelming feeling that somewhere there must be a grown-up who would come and be in charge and make sure he and we were OK. But basically the buck was going to stop with us, and that was a very powerful feeling.

Luckily what may or may not have been a bit of the baby blues passed and in the first few weeks, the fear of not being able to look after this tiny person went away.

What I was left with was what I can only describe as a mildly obsessional love for Billy. Even now that he is eighteen and incredibly annoying at times, I probably have to admit that mildly obsessional love would still be a good way to describe how I feel when I look at him.

As I have said before, I'm fundamentally greedy so more babies were definitely on the horizon. I figured six would be a good number – after all, the Waltons had seven and theirs seemed a positively perfect existence, what with their happy extended family of dungaree-clad grandparents.

The grandparents were always on hand to offer salient advice to the buck-toothed, grass-chewing children about everything important, from the skills of fixing a broken engine to fishing.

Most importantly, I now realise they all had *time* for each other. Time to bake a cake or just eat together or help round up the escaped chickens together. Their tasks and crises were invariably bite-sized and so utterly joyously solvable. No one died unless they were horrible, and no one knew that character anyway. They were a unified joyous hub, where playing their out-of-tune piano in their kitchen passed for a 'cracking event'.

It came as something of a shock that having loads of children wasn't quite as idyllic as it seemed on *The Waltons*. In fact, I would go so far as to say the show was positive misinformation!

The first few years with children are definitely hard, but they do eventually go to bed (albeit not very easily) and you do generally have a moment around 9 p.m. when you can have a glass of wine and breathe a bit.

I am lucky though in that I don't need much sleep; I have a massive amount of energy and am able to juggle thousands of things at the same time. I was also lucky to have amazing people I worked with who helped keep the plates spinning all over the place when I did take my eye off the ball. So we kept on going.

When I had our fourth son, Laurie, Graham and the three older boys, aged five, three and one, came to collect us from hospital. We strapped them all into their four car seats in the back of our seven-seater car and Graham turned to me and said: 'There's room for one more.' My heart sang a little. Yeah, I thought, *The Waltons* here we come.

It turned out he was joking – four sons were enough for him. He told me I could have the rest of my children with my next husband, and I didn't figure anyone would have me now I had four children so I thought I'd better quit whilst I was ahead!

In many ways I think I was well prepared for raising boys as, whilst I had my mother for ten years and my stepmother from the age of twelve, the constants in my life had always been two men – my father and brother. They were joined by my husband as the most significant influences in my life, so adding four more males to the three I'd already got seemed pretty logical.

Having said all that, I think most people just want the children they get. I am sure if I'd had daughters, I would have a very good argument to say I was glad, indeed relieved, I didn't have sons. But I haven't, and life has dealt me the hand it has and I am so unbelievably grateful for it.

There is no doubt to me that, with the odd exception, there are some things that are just consistent with raising boys and some things that are consistent with raising girls. Simply put, my boys need three things: feed them well, sleep them well and exercise them well. Then, much like a dog they are amenable and rather lovely.

Someone once told me girls trash your head and boys trash your house. Well, at your peril would you leave boys who haven't been exercised in a house. The result is not dissimilar to leaving a puppy at home and going to work all day.

I grew up wanting to be a boy because boys seemed to be listened to more and be more relevant. They also seemed to have more fun, more options and more opportunities. I also didn't really like silly clothes that meant I couldn't climb trees with my brother. To resolve this unfairness, I ended up working and living in a man's world and that suited me just fine. In fact, it had more advantages than disadvantages and whilst I am so excited every time I hear of a girl studying engineering, I am also rather flattered by a man calling me 'honey' or 'darling' (obviously only in the right context!).

I also think equality needs fewer labels and more 'go with the flow'. So we have brought up my sons in a family where if they want to dress in a skirt that's fine, if they want to wear makeup that's fine, if they want to go out with a girl or a boy that's fine. If they wanted to do any of the historically more female-based jobs, that too, would be fine. I want them to be who they want to be and respect others for what they want to be. I want them to understand how far we have come in terms of equality and be the generation that continues making changes – and, fingers crossed, I think that is what we have done.

But back to my boys. The first decade or so of having them is now a bit of a blur, but I do remember it not all being a utopian dream of loveliness. There were moments of hideous worry when they were ill and moments of hideous tiredness when they didn't sleep. And I still have moments of hideous self-doubt over almost everything I say and do!

The further away we get from those tough years, the more they end up being edited down as no one really wants to hear more than a few minutes if that about your children's childhoods. So each time you mention it, you have to cut more out and, being in control of my own edit as we all are, I could now sum up their childhoods as 'perfect' (which they clearly weren't!).

Either way, they will be able to see for themselves in the large number of photos and videos that I obsessively took following my first bit of parenting advice from a lovely cameraman I worked with when I was pregnant with Billy: 'Just get the footage and photos and don't worry about editing them until later – you can't get the footage later.' It does mean I have over 120,000 photos that need sorting, but it also means that there is ample joyous footage of happy moments that I realise shapes all our memories of what we were all up to. The only downside to this is it looks like I was never on any of our family trips or holidays as I was always behind the camera, so I have less evidence of what a super spiffing mother I was, always there day and night.

Graham was not quite as good at remembering to be a perfect parent on camera, so there is rather more of him shouting at the children than me. With more practice and control of the record button, I was much better at saying lovely, encouraging words of love when the red light was on!

Although once when Graham cycled to the children's Sports Day from work and took a selfie by the finishing line of the egg-and-spoon race and then promptly left again ten minutes later, I did think he took my salient advice a bit too literally.

I look back and think about the things I worried about that I wish I hadn't. Namely, the children not eating their five-a-day or indeed refusing to eat at all. Now I realise that as a general rule, children don't starve themselves. If they are hungry enough they will eventually eat whatever you give them.

The same with liquids – if water is on offer, they will drink it if they are thirsty, even if they'd rather have squash or Coke. They won't hold out long enough for dehydration to kick in as long as water is readily on offer and in a glass next to their meal.

Similarly, if they want to wear pyjamas to the supermarket, or a dress or bat outfit from the dressing-up box, then fine – in the big scheme of things, does it really matter that much?

When it comes to reading it often felt as if we read every book that has ever been published to them for hours every night. The 'trying to skip pages' trick was always caught and, tail between my legs, I would have to start again. Being a reluctant reader myself, I was desperate to engage them in the dark art of enjoying all books – even climbing trees with them at times to read up there and make the book more exciting.

Then there was the 'lie with me' on their bed until they fell asleep. My children mastered the most effective way of making me do this with the very clever phrase: 'I won't ask forever, mum – you'll regret it if you don't lie with me.' Annoyingly they were probably right!

When I think about the reading and the 'lying with' and so many other things now, I think of how the brilliant Michelle Obama would tell her kids to go away and think in their own room, how she didn't need them to like her as she had her own friends. I wish I had learnt this before having children as I would have been a much better parent!

Basically, it's important to remember that the things you worry about when your children are small are all generally pretty small. The problems become bigger as they get bigger when the subjects they choose to study, or more likely fail to study enough, means they cut off career paths you aren't sure they should cut off. That's the time when you have to learn to let go – you have to let them do things on their own, knowing you won't be there to keep them safe. You have to trust that the world out there will watch over them. That others will help to bring up your tiny piece of perfection and that someone is smiling down on them and keeping them out of harm's way.

People do sometimes ask if I miss them being little but apart from the odd moment, I honestly don't miss that period at all. Just as you don't have to share the love you feel for your first child with your second, because you just get more love somehow, you also don't miss the previous stage because the best moments of the next stage are even better.

So through a combination of good fortune and total lack of planning, I have ended up with four mostly gorgeous, though sometimes insufferable, sons – therefore living with five mostly gorgeous, though sometimes insufferable, men.

I don't think I ever really planned to have children, although the clues to me ending up with a large chaotic family are obvious when I think back now. When I was a child, I loved big families and the element of anarchy and maverick rules that surrounded them, and I loved the energy – and the noise.

We had a couple of family friends when my mother was alive who seemed to me to have children, adults and animals all over the place – spilling out of doorways and crammed under beds. They were always the places that I felt very at home.

One family had a large St Bernard dog which, whilst admittedly a little smelly, was to me utterly joyous.

I can't recall her name but she lay by the large range cooker in what I remember to be a totally ENORMOUS kitchen–living room (that was perhaps not as large as I was small). We all used to lie on top of this massive, giant, warm, and sometimes a little damp and honestly slightly smelly, furry beanbag.

It planted the seed of thought that not only were my parents really unreasonable for not getting such a dog, but also that the minute I grew up and got my own home I would get my own St Bernard.

Once I did have my own house and realised that I'd have to look after this hairy mammoth of a pet, it somewhat took the glow off the idea. Now, inevitably, my youngest son is desperate for the very same dog and he too swears he will get one as soon as he is in 100 per cent control of his pet choices. We shall see.

My other favourite family lived on a farm that I cycled or hacked my rather fat and muddy pony over to. It wasn't a particularly grand farmhouse but there was something so lovely about it and its big farmhouse kitchen complete with an old wood-fired Rayburn.

There was always a couple of cauldrons of stew and mashed potato or similar on the go, ready for all the people who seemed to migrate to the kitchen from around the farm at mealtimes. You'd get into the kitchen through a porch quite literally stuffed full of wellies, coats, riding and farming gear.

Perched amid the piles of slight chaos were also gen-erally several old fruit boxes where the farm cats slept, very often with a litter of kittens.

There is something about baby animals, but especially kittens, that I find irresistible. Someone once told me it's because all baby animals – including humans – have eyes that are out of proportion with their bodies as they don't grow proportionally as much as the rest of their face. So baby animals have oversized eyes which make them very appealing.

I think their soft fur helps as well but also I find the wonderful mix between being utterly helpless and hilar-iously naughty totally enchanting.

Around the time my mother died, I managed to rather cunningly manipulate several of the kittens from the farmhouse back home with me. To be honest, whilst I wasn't really fully aware of what was going on at the time, I was aware that I could ask for almost anything I fancied at that time and generally got it as long as it didn't cost money and wasn't dangerous!

It was this family that my father took me and Diccon to when my mother was in the last few hours of her life and it was there, as the two of us were walking down the farm track, that my father drove up and told us that she was gone.

I hadn't realised she was going to go anywhere so the concept of her dying was a very strange one that I found almost impossible to comprehend. I don't think children can compute something so big and conclusive, so they simply don't.

Rather, it's a slow drip-feed over months, years and decades, getting on with life on a day-to-day basis and stepping over the holes and gaps you come across, unable to get your head round something so significant. However, I will never forget the heartfelt and all-encompassing hug from Janet, who was the mother at the farmhouse, when we were told the news and the awkward but generous warmth from the whole family.

You could tell from the sympathetic, kind eyes that things were not OK. I've always struggled with sympathetic eyes, and I don't know if this is where it came from. For me, 'pity' eyes have always been easy to read and hard to handle.

When it comes to it, you just carry on functioning in this sort of situation. It's not that you are numb, you just don't know what you are. For a moment here and there, you are just normal but then everyone else is not.

The only thing I would say I have learnt is that you should never judge someone else's grief. It is not only none of your business, but it is also entirely absurd for anyone to think someone should act in a certain way externally because of something they are feeling internally. The best advice I could give to anyone witnessing this grief is don't judge; be kind and don't offer irritating advice on anything – at all. Most especially, if you're an adult, don't make stupid comments like 'you are too young to remember' or 'you are old enough to remember' or 'you are an age when you will be OK' or 'you will need to look after your father and brother now'.

Just smile, hug and offer biscuits would be my best advice.

I loved this family who looked after me when I needed it – they did just what I needed them to do. Maybe it's this positive association with these families who my mother and us spent time with when we were little that makes me feel so positively about this sort of household chaos, but it always has and still does make me feel at home.

So for me, people coming and going – not knowing if it's going to be six or twenty-six for lunch until the last minute, never being too phased by the expanding numbers – is the food of life.

By the time we bought Rise Hall I had become used to my then extended family – my stepmother had four children who, whilst a bit older than us, were a bit like close cousins and they came with partners and an array of step-uncles and aunts.

In short, the one consistent thing I have liked all of my life is loads of people, lots of noise and the element of pandemonium that usually accompanies it!

I am not sure which came first – me loving this kind of environment from positive things in my childhood or simply this environment being lovely and therefore me loving it. Either way, the end result is wonderful. I totally appreciate that for many, the noise and chaos would be a nightmare, but I think if this is where your 'happy place' tends to be, you inevitably end up surrounding yourself with like-minded people who enjoy the same thing.

Still, until it came to it, I don't think I was massively driven to necessarily *have* my own children. Honestly, I am not 100 per cent sure I really thought about it that much. I was just aware that some of the films I fancied sculpting my life into did require children to be part of them.

I met Graham and thought he was really good-looking. He had long hair, an earring, sang in a band, made me laugh, was loyal, was game on for adventures and never bored me. So, ten years after meeting, we were still together and children had seemed like the logical next step.

14

Extra maths or a childhood spent climbing trees?

The thing about having all these gorgeous children is that you very badly want them to be happy. Largely I wanted them to go to a school where they could get through unscathed and hopefully be encouraged to want to learn in a way that I wasn't. Ideally, I was hoping that school would be the positive place it wasn't for me and would end up with my children having happy lives.

I have always been pretty vocal about school and what I had hoped my children would get out of it. The boys had all spent their first two years of education in an utterly delightful nursery school (where Laurie – in his final year and my eighth year at the Nativity! – had been Joseph, which after years of tax collectors and donkeys whole-heartedly appealed to my tiger parenting despite all the three year olds being pretty baffled by the whole event!!).

My children then had four years each at a school that was quite literally a two-minute walk from our home. It had a big garden, which was rare for London, with a climbing frame and gingham chair covers and whilst I am not sure they learnt much, they were hot on manners and had a sensational music teacher called Mr Smith.

After that, they went to a little school (again hot on manners and again not so hot on academics) but where there was a music building and an art room, and plays were put on regularly. It was definitely not damaging and had an exceptional head, somewhat bizarrely also called Mr Smith!

It was the next move to a senior school when the problems started. Billy had busted a gut and succeeded in getting into a senior school and got a drama scholarship which was brilliant. The plan was for all his brothers to follow but quite quickly I just wasn't sure about our choices.

It wasn't that the school was a *bad* school; I think it just wasn't the right school for Billy at that moment in his life.

I knew things weren't right when he started to regularly come home and have tea and cake with me. Don't get me wrong, it was absolutely gorgeous to do this with him, and for the first two or three times I thought I'd died and gone to heaven as we sat either side of the kitchen worktop chatting about life in general.

But then a niggling thought came to me that he shouldn't be wanting to spend so much time with me – he should be wanting to spend more time at school with friends or in the endless clubs available.

Things didn't quite stack up.

He wasn't flying in the subjects he loved. I think the school was so big that it had somehow been forgotten that he had a drama scholarship; there seemed to be few opportunities for him to get involved in acting. He played the saxophone and piano pretty well at the time, but didn't really get a chance to play either of them at school. In fact, when he did leave after one year, I talked to the school about this and they said they hadn't realised he played any instruments (it was on his application form so I'm not sure how they missed it).

In short, I think he didn't have the confidence when he arrived to make sure he was noticed for all the right reasons and this, so he claims, was his failing. Personally, I think the school could perhaps have had a system where this sort of information was made known when a new child arrives at the school, but I am proud of Billy for not blaming anyone else for his time not being completely fulfilling at that school.

Meanwhile, our next son, Charlie, was in the throes of applying to the same school. I suspected he would probably get in with a music or drama scholarship, but I wasn't sure it was a school that would be very encouraging in music and drama judging from Billy's experience, and I couldn't see our children becoming more academically motivated or Graham and I being able or wanting to continue pushing them. They had all one by one been diagnosed with dyslexia and that in itself would make it harder.

Then there was our third son, Raffey, to think about. There were different entry stages to the school, and we decided that it might be better for Raffey to start at the bottom aged ten, instead of thirteen, which Billy did.

When we had first spoken to the admissions person, he had been utterly charming – we liked him very much and had made it clear when Billy applied for the school that we had three other sons and expected them all to be going there as well.

We also made it clear that our next two sons were both a bit more dyslexic and whilst they were pretty good at the arts and playing music, and were keen on drama, they weren't massively big readers and academia in its current form was not something either of them particularly flourished at.

With Billy already at the school, I was told that – contrary to what we were first told – it was not really a place that wanted to accommodate arts-focused dyslexic boys, and that, whilst they could probably have got in with enough exam cramming, it probably wasn't the best school for all of the boys.

When I tried to talk to one teacher about it, she suggested the solution was to spend less time doing all of the 'out of school' theatre, music and filming that they did really well – and loved – and spend the time instead focusing on the subjects they were less able at such as science and maths.

It seemed very odd to stop doing the things they were good at and enjoyed to focus on the things they were not very interested in and not so good at. But that was our only option if we were to get them into the same school as Billy. I couldn't stand the thought of spending every weekend having the children tutored and, although everyone assured me at the time that this 'was the norm', it didn't feel very normal to me.

A stolen childhood not spent climbing trees or exploring the world out there just to get 'into' an educational establishment didn't make any sense to me! Particularly as the school Billy had worked so hard to get into didn't seem such a great fit for him after all.

Graham had already said to me when Billy went there, 'What if it's not right for the other boys?' I had replied, 'Well we'll have to move to where there is the right school then.'

It just so happened that the farm Graham and I had casually looked at a couple of years before on a jolly in Somerset was near to somewhere that appeared to me to have the same outlook on education I did: that is, that the five fingers of education, namely academics, music, art, drama and sport, were all as relevant as each other.

Those things seemed to me to be much more reflective of the opportunities out there and were the things I knew the boys all thrived at.

15

Cappuccinos, a stream and a total absence of smelly cows

So that was a deciding factor in moving to Somerset. Not for a nice-coloured kitchen or great wallpaper or a pretty garden, but because it felt like the right thing to do for our family.

That's not to say I didn't still have my doubts about country life as I was still somewhat scarred by the experience of visiting the Smelly Cow Farm, as the children dubbed it, some years before.

This was on another of our many outings to view properties.

It was the middle of winter and the elderly couple who lived there were seemingly marooned in their decrepit static home in the middle of the farmyard. There was literally no hard standing and so, as the cattle were brought in and out to be milked, the combination of their spade-sharp feet and incontinence, plus the rain, meant that, even with wellies on, the mud (and worse) was so deep that it reached up to our knees. Wading through the mud seemed to be a daily normality to the owners as it reached right up to their mobile home door and as far as the eye could see in all directions.

Now I may have been brought up in the country, but I don't ever remember enjoying getting my wellies stuck as a child. In fact, I remember making a terrible fuss when I got stuck fast. You had only one option left and that was to evacuate your foot from the boot and take the inevitable next step in your sock, hoping that the suction effect of the mud was less effective on a more agile sock-covered limb.

We didn't buy the Smelly Cow Farm – apart from the fact it was incredibly stinky, I am secretly a little bit scared of cows. As a child I always had been, but even more so after we had looked at another farm and the farmer showing us round told me he used to have three brothers but two had been tragically killed by the cows – in two separate incidents.

There and then, wading through mud at the Smelly Cow Farm, I resolved I would never cross the line of having to handle something so large and uncontrollable and – to be honest – smelly!

So when Graham seriously suggested buying the farm that would eventually end up being home, I was no more convinced by it than any of the other farms we had seen over the years. But, as Graham generally makes me laugh and is very good company, it was a good excuse to have a couple of hours in the car with him as well as a day in the country.

My first impression of it was not great. I couldn't understand why Graham seemed so delighted with it – there were very few trees and no ancient buildings, be they the existing farmhouse or any other farm buildings.

Worryingly though, he now seemed more excited about this farm than any of the others we had seen. I think he had worked out, which I definitely hadn't, that I was more likely to enjoy the location of this particular farm. It was only about five minutes off a major A road, yet you couldn't hear the traffic. It was less than two hours by car or train to London, Bristol and Bath. And, crucially, it was only thirty minutes from my brother and his family. It was surrounded by towns and villages with interesting theatre, music, art, restaurants and cafés, as well as endless schools catering to incredibly diverse interests and abilities.

With hindsight, Graham's vision was right, which is very annoying, and it was true that trees and hedgerows could be planted, and new houses that you actually really love can be built.

But what he was more right about than I'd ever appreciated is that slowing down and letting things take a bit more time is actually not as boring as I'd thought.

Still, when I first saw the farm, albeit non-muddy, it didn't really float my boat. It had very, very few trees. Granted, it did have a few hedgerows, but they had been hard-trimmed, leaving only the odd lucky tree poking out that had escaped the ruthless flailing machine.

It did have a farmhouse, but it was a 1970s farmhouse with a garden that was utilitarian, not the overgrown wilderness of my dreams, which was much more along the lines of *The Secret Garden*.

It had stock fencing, which is wire squares of fence with two lines of barbed wire above, around a small, mowed patch of grass, the house and the fifty-acre field surrounding it.

If a tumbleweed had rolled in front of the view, it wouldn't have surprised me.

It wasn't a horrible house – just a little bit like the houses you drive past on the side of a main road in France: non-descript with gardens which have so little planted in them that they are really just a place to park the car alongside a bit of not-very-healthy-looking semi-mown grass.

That in itself I could handle, but the barns were all disused, semi-derelict steel-and-corrugated-iron farm buildings with all the romance of steel-and-corrugated-iron farm buildings. There was not a beautiful stone barn or a wrought-iron staircase in sight.

You see, in my head, I had a tick list for a house we might end up living in. It went a bit like this:

1. A walk to a nice pub.

2. Less than two hours to London.
3. Not too far from a town where you can get anything you need, most importantly a decent cappuccino.
4. Woods to walk and play in.
5. Most importantly though, I wanted water – ideally a bubbling river like the one we had by the house I grew up in, where we spent day after day fishing, wading through, swimming in, boating on and generally messing about in.

This farm didn't have this river.

It did, however, have one saving grace. It had a stream, which whilst it wasn't exactly boatable, was a stream nonetheless. And whilst it didn't have a proper wood either side of the stream, it was at least lined with mature trees. In short, it did have a magical something about it.

It also had a lot of concrete hard standing which meant it wasn't too muddy. And no scary cows. It *used* to be a dairy farm in a former life but now had sheep which, having done a lambing season in New Zealand in my late teens, seemed a lot more manageable to me. In truth my lambing experience didn't mean much apart from being able to pull stuck lambs out of a sheep when they gave birth and a few other canny tricks to do with bailer twine and prolapses that should only go into your head on a need-to-know basis.

The real selling point though was the fact that my

brother, his wife, Caroline (Graham's sister), and my beloved three nephews and niece had moved from about half a mile away from us in London to Somerset a few years before. They had moved when all their stars had aligned and their reasons not to move to the place they had always dreamt of had run out.

We had the consolation of having their two eldest sons staying with us whenever they returned to London, which was joyous, but the truth was I missed having us all together. So much so that we had to do regular 'phoners with wine', which is effectively like going to the pub but down the phone – something that certainly wouldn't have happened when I was a child and phone calls were a billion pounds a minute or however much it was that meant I was always being told to get off the phone.

Moving to the farm would mean that we would be delightfully close to them again.

There was my father to think about too. He'd had a stroke three years earlier and I had become increasingly aware that the journey to and from London and indeed just being in London at all was too much for him. For us to help more we needed to be as country-based as he was.

Lastly there was Graham's mother, who had recently been widowed and was West Country-based too.

All this added to the fact that Graham had *always* made it 100 per cent clear that he couldn't imagine – and had no intention of – growing old with pavements out-side his home.

This farm ticked all his boxes. He wanted to have land, to plant trees and watch them grow, and to build a house that finally used up all the contents of his head that he had been collecting over the years about 'the perfect house'.

I guess I felt that it seemed a little churlish to stand in the way of his dream as not only had he never stood in the way of any of my dreams but also the more I looked at the farm, the more the reasons for moving to it stacked up.

Not only was it close to the school that I thought would be good for the boys, but it was surprisingly quick to get back into London. And yes, absurd as it sounds – but it did make a difference to me – there was a farm shop with a restaurant next door that sold really nice cappuccinos in really beautiful cups.

There was even a really great local pub within walking distance.

I was sold.

16

Another new home and another toast with the people I love

The truth is that a home for six people is much more complicated than a home for one, and trying to make the move work for everyone was the biggest juggle I'd ever undertaken.

First, we needed to get the boys on board – the lure of their uncle, aunt and cousins nearby was pretty instrumental in that, together with the fact they were currently at all-boys schools and if we moved they would be going to a school with girls.

Graham did some deals with the boys to get it over the line that, now that I think about them, he still hasn't delivered on – a pair of Timberland boots for Billy if Billy would work his magic on me and deliver me to the plan; he threw in a pygmy goat for me for Billy to trade with. Any final wobbles about leaving London life behind were ironed out by agreeing that our then eight, ten, twelve and fourteen-year-old sons would be allowed to drive on the farm.

My mother Ann, Diccon, me and our family cat Thomas in 1974, in the garden of our childhood home.

A very happy me aged nineteen, standing outside the very first flat we ever bought in Battersea, South London.

The hallway of Rise Hall, which we bought in 2000 –
which, believe it or not, we saw so much potential in.

Billy, aged four weeks, vying for
attention with my beloved cat Alley
– and aged two below, playing the
grand piano at Rise Hall, already a
rock star in the making.

A bitterly cold Rise Hall in the winter of 2008. Boys sledging, with a bit of help from Graham on the lawn-mower!

Rooms restored to their former glory at Rise Hall.

The library at Rise Hall. We loved it so much that we recreated it when we built our home in Somerset.

Our home in South London, at the beginning of our extension work.

Billy, Charlie, Raffey and Laurie getting stuck into building work during a break from football.

The sheep we looked after for Gordon Ramsay, busy eating and destroying our lawn.

Our London home in all its finished glory. We were very sad to lock the door on it for the last time after fourteen wonderfully happy years.

Me pregnant with Laurie, minutes before I left for hospital to give birth to him.

Working mum, here I am at a conference delivering a speech on e-commerce with babe in arms.

Not sure who is more feral – Daisy, our dog, or Charlie aged two.

My four smiling boys pictured here in my dad's pram,
from when he was a baby.

The Entitled Sons, the band formed by my
sons, Graham and our friend Sydney,
performing for crowds.

A blank canvas . . . The field in Somerset before we dug the foundations for our new home.

Finished at last. A new home for new memories.

So we made the leap and moved to Somerset.

I tried not to allow myself to think along the lines of 'what have we done?'. I've always thought it's important to never look back. That is clearly easier said than done sometimes but I have always thought it's a matter of choice whether you dwell on the past, present or future.

It wasn't always easy not to think about what we were leaving behind, but in some ways it was harder for Graham than me because he had been the one trail-blazing all elements of the move. Any imperfections or things that went wrong – which mainly involved me finding it hard – were hard on him.

He did say to me that he was surprised that I hadn't jumped on board immediately and wasn't loving it as quickly as he expected me to do. I did get there – it's just that this time it took a bit longer.

When we'd moved in the past, I'd never had quite so many people I was worrying about. That, together with heading towards fifty, with the hot flushes and irrational moods that comes with that age, made me a bit weaker emotionally than I had been before. But I think I am lucky because despite everything I have an ability to keep walking forward when things aren't so perfect.

Once we had bought the farm and moved – imperfect as it may have been at the time – we had a plan and we had to keep going. When you walk through mud – if you keep going you will eventually get to the other side.

Sooner or later, it will be a sunnier day but *only* if you keep moving forward.

I also think I'm lucky in that one of my most fortunate characteristics is to have never blamed anyone other than myself for events in my life. Owning your decisions and events in your life empowers you to be in control. So that's what I did.

Practically and emotionally, I tore up my little black book. Back in London, I had a shorthand enabling me to run our lives and fit a massive amount in. I had lots of friends I could rely on who lived just around the corner. I knew where to get things, who to call out or see, from fixing the dishwasher to where to buy milk at 11 p.m. on a Sunday night. I knew where to go for Sunday lunch or coffee on a Tuesday morning. I knew most of the local shopkeepers and the man who ran the fruit stall in the market. I knew where to get my dry cleaning done if I was in a hurry and who to get to fix the car. We had a great family doctor and dentist too.

Life was delightfully familiar; everywhere I turned it felt comfortable. I had a sense of belonging and that brought with it an ease to life that I knew I'd only really appreciate once I didn't have it to fall back on.

Moving to Somerset, the administration of life was completely thrown up in the air, from changing addresses on all documentation involved in our extremely complicated lives to getting four lots of new school uniform and sewing name tapes in them all.

We were also kissing goodbye to the boys' *amazing* piano teacher, Nicole, who had been so utterly instrumental in them working their way up to the grades they were at.

We were kissing goodbye to the fantastic theatre where both Billy and Charlie had performed in the East End of London.

We were kissing goodbye to last-minute 'let's pop out to supper' moments on a random week night.

It wasn't that any of this stuff was impossible to get over – it was more the sheer quantity of things that we were leaving that was so very overwhelming. But we all learn lessons through adversity and I learnt so much.

I learnt I was luckier than I ever realised because you can make fun in any situation if you want to enough.

The first night we moved in, Diccon, Caroline and their children came over to celebrate.

Amazingly, we found a local Indian takeaway that delivered – though when it arrived they only took cash, which meant we had to raid every corner of every car, coat and bag to scrape enough money together to pay for it!

Much like we had so many years before in Rise, and before that, when we'd bought our very first flat together, we all sat in the garden and toasted our new adventure – drinking out of my charity shop pottery wine glasses and eating rice and curry with teaspoons because we could only find side plates to eat off (and really small ones at that).

Years before, I remember Graham and I helping Diccon and Caroline pack all their luggage and their four young children into their car after Christmas and new year at Rise Hall. In it all went and, as the last door slammed shut and they pulled away, Graham turned to me with a smile and said, 'That's a party on wheels.' Nothing has ever quite summed up how I feel about large families better. None of the complications of our first night mattered because the truth is when we are all together, and then also have Diccon and his family, everyone has a wonderful knack of making almost any situation feel a bit like a party. I already thought I was pretty lucky in the first place, but I learnt that, trite as it might sound, home really is where the people you love are.

Lastly, I learnt that a new adventure only starts when you take a risk – inertia is something that comes upon you slowly like a morning fog. It holds you in a safe, comfortable place, but if it's an adrenaline-filled ride you want, then inertia, whilst it may feel like a hot chocolate and duvet at the time, is in fact your arch-enemy.

17

A TV snug, two dishwashers and a four-man jacuzzi

There was certainly no chance of inertia in those first few weeks and months after moving to Somerset. We were adjusting to living in a new house and an unfamiliar area, whilst the boys were having to settle in at a new school. There was also the small matter of designing, getting planning permission for, and building our new home.

Between us, Graham and I have around 100 years of experience of living in homes but also changing homes, building homes and creating homes. Add in our four children's 'relevant' opinions, and it's around 150 collective years of experiences of 'homes'.

So it would be odd if after all that – together with a Covid lockdown hitting, meaning we were all stuck together – we couldn't create a family home that was pretty spot on in terms of working perfectly for all our family.

We each had our 'wish lists'. I was pretty attached to

our home in London but when we broke it down, it was only bits of that home I really loved – other bits I was quite happy to leave behind.

There was one particular downstairs room in our London home that I loved. The house had been added to in pretty odd ways over the last 150 years, so there was the addition of a bay window and a set of French doors (that are actually called French windows but if you call them that no one knows what you are talking about). It wasn't so much the room but more the memories of it that I loved: a small, cosy snug off the kitchen that we used to watch TV in. It was indeed a 'happy place' for me.

So when Graham drew the first blueprints of our new home and I, rather grumpily I fear, said, 'Well it doesn't have a TV room like our house in London,' Graham duly went back to the drawing board and returned with new plans that included a room that was pretty much identical in size.

At the time he did say he couldn't see why I wanted it, but it turned out we now use this room all the time. I try not to point out how right I was too much. The point is Graham tried so, so hard to meet everyone's needs when designing our new home. For him it was a dream that was a long time in the making and I think he wanted all of us to want it as much as he did, so he bent in whatever ways he could to accommodate all our demands.

One side of the house, the west side, was designed especially for me. The style of this side of the house leans much further toward the Victorian 'chaotic' addition-based façade that you might have got with an older house that has evolved over generations.

That's because I love old houses and the stories they tell – this family at one time lived there and then this family moved in and did this to the house for this reason, etc. A new house has no history, but we could at least design in those quirky things that aren't truly symmetrical or totally planned. I like the little oddities of a house that has evolved and the Victorians were masters of this.

For the first time in the Industrial Revolution, more normal people had money to spare. In many ways it was the birth of consumerism in its modern form, when people had the money to buy things they wanted rather than buy things they needed. So they often extended their homes – just because they could.

And it wasn't just a handful of the super-rich that were doing this. Many of the working classes were suddenly lifted off the breadline and became the new burgeoning middle class. There were thousands of them and they, in their thousands, built new homes, refurbished old ones, built elaborate new fronts and backs on houses and con-structed staff wings.

This was when things were mass-produced for the first time, with more than a few people having money to spare, trinketry was on everyone's shopping list. I love all periods of history, but I do love some of the nonsense that was built in the Victorian times because of the eccentricity – and I really wanted some reflection of this period in the house we were creating.

As for the other quirks:

I wanted a secret room, Graham drew one in. I wanted a secret door, Graham drew one in. I wanted a walk-in larder, Graham drew one in.

The kids' favourite part of Rise Hall was being able to rollerblade around the house in a circuit – so he designed one in. They also loved being able to chase each other up and down the many staircases there – Graham didn't quite manage the seven that we had at Rise Hall, but he put two in so they could run up one and down the other.

When it came to their bedrooms, the kids were given a totally free rein. This might sound insane but we had three reasons behind this:

1. We had made so many decisions we literally had decision fatigue.
2. We wanted the children to have ownership of the new house, especially their bedrooms, as by the time it was finished we didn't want them to feel they were camping for a bit in their parents' house before leaving home.
3. We had a load of furniture from Rise Hall that had been carefully put together for the bedrooms there but the new owners didn't want it, so the children had a narrower choice of furniture options based on 'what we already had'!

In the end their rooms turned out to be just what we wanted them to be – and that is what *they* wanted them to be. In fact, looking at it now, I think we got the build of our home pretty spot-on for all of us.

As we were building from scratch, we were even able to consider where the sun rose and set, so now I have the luxury of watching the sun rise in my bedroom every morning whilst drinking a cup of tea. We built an airing cupboard with a warm loop of pipe to keep the damp out of the sheets. We built a kitchen with two dishwashers and all the cupboards to empty them. We put sockets on the kitchen island so when you want to charge something you don't have to trip over a trailing cable.

We even put a cupboard in the utility room with loads of chargers and a lock on the door so it was possible to lock devices away. Alas, this works better in theory than practice as the children are older now and less amenable to the 'remove devices' parenting – and anyway they quickly worked out how to pick the lock.

Although we did get one thing wrong. Or should I say, *I* got one thing wrong. We had a bathroom in Rise Hall that had two baths. It was a bit of a hangover from its previous function as a school, but when we refurbished the room, we put two baths side by side in the middle of the room with taps at either end. This was largely because Graham and I love baths rather than showers, and he found my bath too hot and I found his bath too cold so, as a wedding present to ourselves, we did up the bathroom and for a year or so had luxurious times with a bath each and a glass of wine each. This stopped when the children started arriving and we no longer had time to do this!

The year I was pregnant with Billy I had twenty-six really good friends who were also pregnant, so a year or so later our luxury pair of baths were often literally stuffed full of children, watched by an array of designated parents sitting like wallflowers on various chairs around the edge of the room – all with a glass of wine in hand. I have dozens of photos of the children I love most in the world getting older year by year sitting in those bathtubs.

I wanted to copy this bathroom in our new house. I recognised that the children were too old for the mass bath time but figured it was still sociable for people to be able to bathe together and when grandchildren arrived, we could pick up where we left off.

Incidentally, you should *always* design a home for ten years' time and not right now, so I was thinking ahead. However I made a mistake with this bathroom though – I meant to try and find one of those big corner 1970s jacuzzi baths, which I figured would serve the same purpose as two tubs, as the room just wasn't big enough for two baths like Rise Hall. Instead I found a four-man circular jacuzzi bath and, with zero support from Graham, went and bought it without him knowing a thing about it.

When the jacuzzi finally arrived months later, we had to take the walls out to get it to the top floor. Once in place, the walls were rebuilt and it was literally embedded there. It would need to be chopped in half to ever get it out, it was at this point it dawned on me that it uses about five normal bath-fulls of hot water. This I hadn't considered.

So not my finest idea, though for now it's fun used every now and then, but probably if I'm honest comes under the heading of 'stupid ideas of Sarah's', most of which I like to sweep quickly under the carpet.

18

A dining table with a rock 'n' roll history and a very special sideboard

Having had Rise Hall for twenty-odd years, I don't think it's very surprising that so much of our new home was inspired by it, but our dining room really is the summation of all our dining room dreams.

Rise Hall was a house of parties. You wouldn't buy a house with ninety-seven rooms, thirty-two of which were bedrooms, if you didn't want lots of people to come and stay.

From early on at Rise, we had sit-down dinners. First on a load of trestles from Ikea with a huge long piece of plywood on top with slightly rounded corners. This was finished off with a piece of curtain lining that covered for a damask tablecloth.

And then, about ten years ago, we were given one of our very favourite pieces of furniture: a massively long, and very, very beautiful Victorian dining table. It was a gift from Jo Wood, from the days when she and her then-husband Ronnie had had a much bigger dining room.

Jo had emailed my agent out of the blue to say she had watched our TV show on renovating Rise Hall and would we like their old table for our dining room. It was such a gorgeous, generous thing to do, and we very gratefully accepted it.

When I finally met Jo a few years later, she was so joyously warm and bubbly. I interviewed her for my podcast series, *Round the Houses*, which was one of the most enjoyable things I've ever done. It involved talking to some of the nation's treasures, fascinating people like Julian Clary, Pearl Lowe, June Sarpong, Joe Sugg, Lynn Bowles and Tim Lovejoy, who told me about their lives as they showed me around their homes.

It was a bit of a window into radio, which I totally love listening to and secretly feel I have very unfinished business with.

Anyway that was how I met Jo, and I ended up spending a very enjoyable afternoon learning all about her rather amazing organic beauty products, her home and her life. She is just as beautiful on the inside as the outside, which is always wonderfully un-disappointing!

Once we had the fabulous dining table, which probably had a more colourful life in its last home with Jo and Ronnie, we knew we would have to build a dining room around it in Somerset. So we did just that. The length and width of the room was designed specifically around the table, along with the beautiful sideboard that Graham's parents bought us for a wedding present. If we hadn't had Rise Hall, the sideboard would have been a very weird present, but with a massive dining room that needed filling, it was perfect.

Many would call it a big bit of useless brown furniture, but we love it. It is about eight feet long, made of mahogany, and has a drawer in the middle for cutlery that has the remnants of the dark green velvet that it was once upon a time carefully lined with. It has a cupboard at each end. One cupboard has shelves and the other has a shelf at the top and then a drawer underneath with little square holes you can slot decanters into, each of which is lead-lined.

This makes the sideboard very heavy but also always makes me wonder who would have been in charge of putting the bottles into it all those years ago – how they would have dressed and thought and spoken, which house the piece of furniture was in and what tales it would tell if it could.

This sideboard has seen us through twenty years of our life; this and the dining table were very worthy items to build our new dining room around.

The dining room is probably one of the most convincing old (new) rooms in the house. It has a fine open fireplace made by a company called Jamb that I have always admired. They had a fireplace that had been made for somebody who had changed their mind, so we got it at a really good price. The ceiling and walls have highly decorative plasterwork in panels that would have been gold leaf in the past, but we found a mix of two gold paints from Ardenbright that gave a believably similar effect at an awful lot cheaper cost.

The plasterwork itself was not designed for the room but instead made by chopping up and sticking together different moulds from a variety of plaster companies. Graham is king and master of detailing and never ever gets it wrong, so I was only too happy to stay well out of this.

The walls are a dark, dusty green and the curtains of gold silk are more Rise Hall cast-offs.

But it is the table and the sideboard, and the stories that come with them, that make it such a special room for me. In fact, we have bits of sentimental furniture dotted all over the house, each with their own story and each one making us smile. I have a tiny Victorian red velvet nursing chair and a dressing table that belonged to my paternal grandmother. It now lives in the corner of my bedroom, and I sit at it every morning and watch the beautiful sunrise.

I actually have a bit of an obsession with red velvet. From Victorian theatres to Victorian sofas, I can't think of anywhere or anything that an armful of dark red velvet doesn't look utterly fabulous on. (Although Graham's mother would disagree – she tells me that my red velvet obsession tips a little into a Victorian brothel interior.)

In our bedroom we have a bed that we built from MDF and painted for Rise Hall when we designed a

Georgian bedroom there for a series we made for television about the history of Christmas.

We have a gorgeous writing desk that my first lovely stepmother left me in her will. It's a beautiful, big, heavy mahogany writing bureau with a fold-down writing table. Inside it has little secret drawers that always fascinated me when I was a teenager.

On the walls we have framed pictures of various relatives from decades gone by. I find it very comforting to have them staring down from their perches – as if they are still looking out for all of us. I also have a collection of expired passports, which in my opinion are a fascinating piece of history in themselves.

Then there are a few really weird things like my late mother's wisdom teeth and my father's broken pipe – they were legacies I inherited and struggle to make myself throw away.

And, although I try hard not to, I can't seem to resist adding to this bizarre collection of family memorabilia. I have kept the hair from all my sons' first haircuts as well as all their baby teeth.

At least these I can justify as being cute as they're often paired with very sweet letters to the tooth fairy and duly written replies carefully crafted in my version of 'fairy writing', whereas my mother's teeth I imagine were brutally extracted when she was a fully grown adult at some point and for some reason handed back to her.

It's the only piece of DNA I have of her forty years

later and, for some weird, macabre reason, this single fact justified her wisdom teeth being moved into our new home and squirrelled away into a top cupboard in the hope I won't have to face the inevitable moment when I have to actually discard them.

It could be worse. I have dealt with a massive amount of this kind of stuff over the years. Luckily, the tea chest of stained, twice-used Terylene nappies from me and my brother's childhoods has gone.

I also inherited the top layer of my parents' wedding cake, which lived in a tin on the upper shelf of the larder at our childhood home. My brother and I, who were brought up largely sweets-free, would climb up, remove the lid and sneakily pick off the decorative icing to eat bit by bit.

By the time my mother died, the cake must have been a good eighteen years old and by the time my father carefully passed it on to me at Rise Hall, it was probably thirty-five years old. It then lived in Rise Hall for a few years until our eldest son, Billy, was born and, the cake having missed my brother's christening all those decades earlier, Diccon and I decided to celebrate not by eating (unsurprisingly) but by throwing the cake into the lake. We figured making 'an event' of the its disposal somehow made it more acceptable, even if it did have a smack of a Viking burial about it.

So there we were, with our father, all dressed in our Sunday best, slightly absurdly but very joyously ceremonially breaking off pieces of cake and throwing it into the lake!

I promised myself that I would try not to leave my children any such items that they would have to unburden themselves of later down the line, though fortunately they seem utterly baffled by my sentimental nonsense so perhaps they are cured of it already!

The remainder of the weirdest things we own we have put into the downstairs loo, which is probably the best place for all items you don't quite know what to do with. These include the Victorian stuffed animals given to us over the years, as well as my father's gas mask from the war, although sadly the rubber is definitely on its way out.

Our stuffed animal collection

Rise Hall is responsible for all sorts of things and one of those is our stuffed animal collection.

Having ninety-seven empty rooms with empty walls to fill meant Rise became a useful receptacle for all those things our friends and family didn't want to throw away – but didn't want to keep either.

We have a great friend Geoffrey who works for an auction house. It is partly him who started the 'stuffed animal' collection, as somewhat unsurprisingly the random and often weird stuffed animals tend to be left unsold at the end of auctions and can be picked up for a few pounds.

With great delight hc bought a Victorian stuffed badger in a glass case, which he gave to me as a birthday present. And then that Christmas, my brother Diccon found a stuffed crocodile collecting dust at the back of an old junk shop that he gave to Raffey, who liked crocodiles (but probably alive not dead, and this one had been dead for a good hundred years!).

Then came the owl, various deer heads and a water buffalo head (really weird and MASSIVE!) that came from my parents-in-law's great friends who had a restaurant where it lived on the wall. When they sold the restaurant, they kindly popped it in the back of my in-laws' car and they promptly drove it up to Rise Hall.

My in-laws had a Border Terrier at the time called Percy, who assumed the ear of the buffalo was actually a bit of biltong, and by the time it arrived in East Yorkshire part of it had been consumed!

19

Beware the yellow Ferrari haters

We always knew it would be tricky to get planning permission to build a new house in the countryside. That is regardless of your design, as of course design is subjective and what is 'beautiful' or 'not beautiful' is in the eye of the beholder.

Graham and I love all forms of architecture from medieval castles to minimalist brutalism, but honestly I think our favourite is classical architecture and if you are going to build a home to live in, then obviously it makes more sense to build a home you like looking at and living in. I think that with design, the best of the old comes forward and stands the test of time. The stuff that is a bit of a weird momentary flight of fancy in terms of design will not last and in fifty years will be demolished and replaced with something else.

In 2012 I jointly curated an exhibition about the Home at RIBA (Royal Institute of British Architects) that spelt out really clearly the journey of 'the home' over the last 250-odd years.

What was so interesting to me was that 'design' as we currently know it really largely came about after the Second World War. That's when the role of an 'architect' became something independent from either an artist, who came up with the concept of the overall vision of a home, or the builder who was going to build it.

Post-war, this new group of people – who often neither had to pay for the buildings to be built, or be answerable to the people who were paying for them, owning them, or living in them – were asked to design homes. Architects.

It was around this time that think-tanks on conceptual living became a 'thing' and rows of terraced inner-city homes were replaced with tower blocks to provide larger communal space for people to share, rather than little back yards for people to have for just their own use.

In fairness to these blue-sky thinkers, the housing that was being demolished was often 'slums' with poor sanitation and bustling overcrowding – not the quaint Victorian terraces that we often see today. But it was the architecture that was perceived to be largely at fault.

One thing I do believe is that a building should always be built to last. A goodly lump of the earth's resources will have been put into manufacturing the materials, shipping them to a site and then constructing a building.

It should therefore be built in a design that is likely to stand the test of time and it should be built to be sturdy enough to withstand the ravages of Mother Nature over hundreds of years. We all now know that disposable is not good for the planet – and 'disposable' homes are no different.

Anyway, back to Somerset. We knew that getting planning permission to build a new home in the country would be a lengthy if not impossible process, so we bought a farm that already had planning permission to build a new home. The permission was not quite for the home we wanted to build but for a similar-sized one on the same farm.

We are lucky enough to live close to a local historical landmark – King Alfred's Tower. This is a 160ft (49m) high folly, designed by Henry Flitcroft for Henry Hoare II in 1772 and it is believed to mark the site where King Alfred the Great rallied his troops in 878. The tower itself commemorates the accession of King George III to the throne in 1760 and the end of the Seven Years' War.

There were a few reasons why we wanted to change the field we were to build our house in and one of them was that, in the new location, the house would be much less visible from the tower.

This is because the new field was much lower down so whilst we benefitted from being 'in a dip', which was more private, so did anyone outside the land, too, by not having their view interrupted. Plus, the house being much lower on the land had another massive advantage – it was next to a little stream.

The farm had had many miles of hedgerows and trees removed after the Second World War when the government had a push to encourage intensive farming to grow enough food to end rationing. So farmers were paid to remove hedgerows and trees in favour of larger fields so big machines could work quicker.

The effect of this has been increasingly felt in the decades since as, with the law of unintended consequences, the impacted and poorer quality soil means that the rain runs across and off the surface of the land rather than soaking into it and slowly seeping through the soil to ditches, rivers and streams. This is because the land is much less porous with no tree roots and hedges to break it up.

This washes the nutrients off the land and into the streams and rivers, but also means that the speed that it runs off the land causes more and more flash flooding downstream.

We had a vision when we bought the farm. We wanted to replace the hedgerows and trees that would have once been there. In short, we wanted to have a farm with a home and garden that helped nature be the best that it could be, so that generations to come would not despair of our period of ownership and wish that we had done something differently that might have helped this beautiful planet we all live on last as long as we can.

In the five years since we arrived, so much has changed. So far we have planted 25,000 mixed British woodland trees and replanted several miles of hedgerows. We have not hard cut the hedgerows we do have and have let Mother Nature take control of the edges of our fields.

It's just a start but even in these very early days we already have a better balance with nature, and the wildlife and plant life has already started to flourish.

When we first moved here it was so utterly silent I almost expected to see tumbleweed whistling across the gargantuan fields. No longer. Now the sound of birds and insects (yes, insects are actually really noisy when there are enough of them in the summer!) are a joy to hear.

There are also so many different wild birds that come to visit and stay that I have had to get my 'book of birds' from my childhood out to identify some of them, and the binoculars are always out and at the ready in our kitchen and bedroom.

With the trees planted, we then turned our attention to building the house. Not just a house but a home. Clearly the act of building a house at all is not the greenest thing to do, but humans need homes and arguably we need more houses to be built. We wanted to build a home that was a legacy to all we had learnt and achieved.

Whilst I feel very lucky that the twists and turns of our lives have led us to where we are, I think I can largely attribute my success to one single factor – I do not make excuses and do not accept them when they are given to me.

What I feel most fortunate for is the ability to take responsibility for my own actions, and for seeing and taking opportunities that have come along. My luckiest twist of fate was, after the one of being born at all, to be born in the UK – my British passport is my most valuable possession. Then there is a massive amount of hard work and determination that ended us up where we are.

I think we have a tendency in this country to allow ourselves to be jealous. I was once told that being jealous is like drinking poison and hoping the other person will die. I tend to call it the yellow Ferrari syndrome.

There are many in this country who, if they saw a yellow Ferrari driving down the road and couldn't buy one themselves, would prefer to have yellow Ferrari's banned because if they can't have one then it doesn't seem right that anyone else should have one either.

I don't subscribe to this theory. I don't have a yellow Ferrari, but I am happy for them to exist and be for sale. In fact, I rather like seeing them being driven down the road or parked somewhere.

We built our home knowing we were always going to have a few 'yellow Ferrari haters' and we did, but fortunately only a handful.

So we all jumped into living in Somerset with both feet and I do feel so very at home here now. We were so, so lucky to be invited to get stuck into life down here so quickly, meeting dozens of neighbours from nearby villages who were utterly lovely.

We were invited to a barbecue by some of our new wonderful neighbours about a week in and had phone calls from two different friends of friends asking us to come for lunch.

I thanked all these families but pointed out there were six of us so it might be best if Graham and I came without the children – but all of them insisted we all come. I am so grateful to them for their generosity at the beginning and all of them are now really good friends.

In fact, we moved in during summer and by Christmas we were all so overwhelmed by the wonderfully kind welcome we'd had, that we invited lots of the people we'd met to a Christmas drinks party (a bit chaotic as we were living temporarily in the 1970s house on the farm). We had masses of bowls of crisps and some slightly burnt mini sausage rolls but it was a fun evening and I reflected on how lucky we were to have found another place to live with so many brilliant, kind, fun and interesting people all around.

20

Lost and found: a very special doll's house

There are plenty of places around the inside and outside of our new home that are unfinished. Our bedroom still has no pictures on the walls. In fact there are pictures that are piled up in corners all over the house with 'going to do' mental memos on them all. Some of the pictures need a bit of restoration or reframing or time to fathom out what or who they are meant to be.

We also made the stupid mistake of taking all the little brass shade rings off all the side lamps when we packed up Rise Hall and our home in London. The shades were all packed together and the lamps all bubble-wrapped in different boxes, but the little shade rings that kept the shades on the lamps went somewhere altogether unfindable.

As a result, we now have two attic cupboards full of lamps in a combination of conditions. Some requiring rewiring were bought in various auctions over the years – but all are shade-free with no one able to remember what might have gone with what and unable to hold them together anyway. I will, one day, get them all out and 'deal' with them – but it's really low on my to-do list!

Somewhere too far, far down on my to-do list is a little tiny dream of mine of having the ultimate 'granddad's' workshop. This is effectively a shed – it's marginally based on Barry Bucknell's DIY TV shows from the 1950s and some set dressing I am sure I saw in something like *Cider with Rosie* or *Last of the Summer Wine*.

My father had a rather similar workshop at the end of our house when I was a child and he, like Barry, would wear a brown pop-together shopkeeper's coat with big square pockets containing sawdust, nails, screws and the odd tool.

I think my heavily disguised OCD quite fancies a wall with carefully lined up tools in size order and, in a perfect world, sprayed with shadow paint to leave no guessing as to which tool was missing should one not be put back.

All this would be in some gorgeous outbuilding with a beaten-up old leather armchair and DEFINITELY the ability to make a cup of tea.

It would have a workbench with a vice attached and a lathe all set up ready to go next to a sharpener for the chisels. It would have a band saw and a drill stand. It would have efficient screw and nail storage, and a little shelf that had various glues, stains, varnishes, WD40 and 3 in 1 oil. In short – if you wanted to fix something, make something or simply imagine that you might do one of those two things, you could visit this space and lay your hands on every item you wanted instantly.

Alas the dream workshop remains just that – a dream – for the moment at least, and certainly very far down my to-do list. There are also areas of the house that are annoying and could be better – despite over-speccing the number of electrical sockets, there are still two places we didn't put them that I wish we had. One in Laurie's bedroom between two windows and one in the library next to the fireplace. The sockets may have been lacking but fortunately, having wired endless houses over the years, we didn't make the silly and expensive mistakes of putting speakers in the ceilings or trying to have dramatic automation or anything.

To be honest, you never realise these things are mistakes until you actually live with them. Remember, everything electrical WILL go wrong at some point – it is inevitable and so just another thing that will need to be fixed. In the meantime, gadgetry is only as good as the user and if you aren't the sort of person who wants to spend hours downloading apps to reset and reschedule turning on your lights instead of just walking in and switching a switch, you're better off steering clear. And as for speakers in the ceiling, whilst amazing in theory, I personally think it's a terrible way to listen to music as it's much more enjoyable to have music coming from one direction. This means you can then step away or closer depending on what you fancy. It's similar to having a fire that you can stand next to or move away from instead of being in a very hot room.

We also somehow managed to put the hardwired Wi-Fi booster in our bedroom on the wrong side of the room, and the TV seems to want a cable as it is reluctant to work remotely on the Wi-Fi. Perhaps when our TV eventually dies a new one will be much improved!!

Also the kitchen needs curtains to make it a bit less echoey and possibly some colour too. I'd love to get more pictures up and possibly hang all the weird kitchen implements we have inherited but don't work as well as modern ones around somewhere. A map and perhaps a chalk board to leave the children lists of things I want them to do that they probably won't do are also on my agenda and a kitchen table that isn't a piece of plywood on trestles with an oil cloth on top.

Our bedroom also still needs curtains too, and we boxed in the chimney flue from the room below, keeping it tight to the pipe instead of building it out to the width of the bedhead. Graham didn't want to waste the space in case we came up with a cunning plan later on – but we are still waiting to have the cunning plan!

But all these unfinished quirks don't matter because, surrounded by the bits and pieces from our past, Somerset now feels very much our home. Our old friends and family find our new house weirdly familiar – which it is. It is all the bits of homes we had before squashed into one – it reflects everything we have loved in our homes. It is all the best bits of Rise Hall, the house we loved so much in London and our camping field with a treehouse all wrapped into one. A new house full of mementos from thirty years of adventures together.

One of the most fascinating things I had to find a home for in Somerset (along with the teeth, my sons' hair, the stuffed animals and the gas mask) was a very special doll's house that I am now the proud owner of. My mother and father had various jobs, one of which was making doll's house furniture.

At the time, they were then commissioned by two separate people to build a full doll's house. One for someone in the United States and one for a lady in the UK called Mrs Abraham, who wanted a copy of her childhood home. I remember going with my parents to deliver the doll's house to her when it was finished; she gave us biscuits and orange juice and her husband showed us his collection of very cool cars.

My parents stayed in touch with Mrs Abraham and then, after my mother died, my father still kept this friendship going. When I was in my late teens, I too ended up writing to her and eventually visiting, and it was on one of these visits that she asked if I would like the doll's house when she died. When I said yes, she promised that she would leave it to me in her will and I was utterly thrilled.

I knew old doll's houses weren't especially valuable as

they took up extra spare space that people no longer had in their homes, but this particular doll's house meant an awful lot to me having been painstakingly built by my parents on the kitchen table over months as we watched. We had a family trip to a slate mine in Wales where we walked into the mine and collected slate, which my father soaked and hand-split to clad the roof with. Years later I visited the same mine which by then was fully automated and bore little resemblance to the couple of old diggers in a hole I remembered. I am not sure if it's just my life or everyone's, but the connections and references from the past come thicker and faster the older you get.

But back to the doll's house. The walls inside were covered in fabric that my mother and I went to London to get from Liberty. It had to be very small print. And I remember too my parents finding wrapping paper with little scenes which they cut out to use as pictures for the walls. My father made little gold frames out of casting plaster that he gold-plated to frame them with. Even the tiny bath taps were cast, and the chair legs carved with a Stanley knife late into the night. My mother plaited cotton to edge the sofas and stitched tiny tapestry rugs.

My parents used to visit various craft fairs where they advertised and displayed the doll's house furniture they made. They had a large frame made of wood then covered in old wallpaper, which looked like a wall but was very light to move. Into this they slotted half a dozen sample rooms. Diccon and I would hide behind it and often try and escape. I remember one fair in a place called Hickstead where the stall next door had made little men from acorns, which I thought were really cool; they gave me one, which I still have somewhere. It is all these memories that meant I loved that doll's house.

Then, about ten years ago, I got a call to say that Mrs Abraham had passed away. I was sad about it as she was incredibly kind, but she was very old. Her equally lovely daughter then said she was so sorry but she had only just found out that her mother had promised the doll's house to me. Unfortunately, however it had been sent to a house clearance auction a couple of weeks before and had been sold.

She very kindly told me the name of the auction house and, as the trail still had a scent, I phoned them to see if they knew who had bought it. When I recounted the story with some excitement, they told me that they knew exactly who had bought it – for £120 with all the furniture inside. They told me they would phone the buyer and ask them if I could buy it back from them. I explained that I would be only too happy to pay the buyer more than they had paid for it, or find them an-other doll's house if they wished in exchange.

I knew that a doll's house is really of little value and that one day, despite the months spent creating it, it would probably end up on a bonfire if it wasn't reunited with someone who it meant a lot to. Sadly, when the auction house phoned me back they told me that the lady who had bought it said under no circumstances would she consider selling it back to me or exchanging it. So I asked if I could perhaps send a little note to her to be kept with the doll's house. The note was a photo of my parents from the *Reading Gazette* that I had kept. It featured them and the doll's house they had made, and I added my contact details and I asked if she could possibly place the note inside the doll's house in the hope that someone at some point in the future would read it and decide not to throw it away but to return it to me.

Then years later, completely out of the blue, I got a call. The lady had decided that as her granddaughter had never showed any interest in the doll's house, she would let me buy it off her after all. In truth I had put this one to bed and didn't really want the doll's house anymore – I had grown to accept that it was gone and we had sold Rise Hall, which would have had plenty of room to devote to a massive collector's doll's house like this. Plus I had four sons who I suspected were all now too old to even consider looking at a doll's house. But of course as I had started this ball rolling so many years before I couldn't possibly refuse and went to collect it.

Sadly, my father who is a bit forgetful now, no longer remembered either the doll's house or making it when I showed it to him. I tried hard to point out how clever he was, but he couldn't accept it was his creation so that ship, too, had sailed. So now I have a MASSIVE doll's

house, which houses so many memories of lovely moments in my childhood, that I am not quite sure what to
do with! It's a lesson to be super-duper careful what you
wish for in life because, as I have discovered, it might all
just come true.

21

Happy Sundays and cool dips in our new ponds

One of the most important things on my tick list for moving to the country was 'water'. Now this could have been a river or it could have been a pond (not a small one but one big enough to swim in and paddle a boat around in) or a lake – just so long as I had somewhere to dip my head under. Because, in the wonderful words of Ratty in *The Wind in the Willows* by Kenneth Grahame: 'There is nothing – absolutely nothing – half so much worth doing as simply messing about in boats.'

My childhood ended up centring around the River Whitewater that ran at the end of our garden. The River Whitewater was shallow enough to stand in most places, though it ranged from knee to chest height. I learnt to swim in the mill pond by jumping off the weir a little upstream, which has resulted in me being fairly bold at jumping off things but not very good at actually swimming any distance! Some of our favourite and best days out as children, and later as young adults, were always on the river.

We had an old plastic blue fibreglass boat my father had got second-hand from somewhere or other and my brother had a canoe that was given to him by my parents for getting a scholarship to secondary school (I didn't get a scholarship or a canoe!). My father would put the boat, my brother's canoe and another canoe he made when he was a teenager onto our old trailer and drive us down a very long farm track near our house to get about five miles upstream. He would then dump us along with all the floating equipment and drive home. Diccon and I and various friends would spend an idyllic day floating, occasionally rowing, downstream. The very shallow bits meant we needed to climb out to make the boats higher in the water or sometimes we'd have to darg or carry them over the gravelly bits – but this just added to the adventure. We also, as we got bigger, generally had a bag of beers that were pulled behind one of the boats to keep cool.

Several hours later, having intrepidly pushed the slightly leaking boats over the weir and happily getting very wet along the way, we'd arrive at the bit of river our garden backed onto, where we would drag out the boats and the bag of empty beer bottles and carry them in squelching wet trainers back home. It is against this background that my vision of childhood sits. So I reckon anyone would understand that when it came to moving to the country, water for me was a must.

So, when Graham showed me the farm he had found and it had a stream, that was a big tick – you can jump in a stream, walk in a stream, dam a stream, sit by a stream – PLUS it had enough trees either side to almost count as woodland (probably a bit of an exaggeration – more like a few trees, but it was better than nothing). But it had a stream – which whilst it may not have been a river, it was definitely not a ditch. Whilst we were walking around the farm for the first time, I realised it was very wet indeed in a lot of the fields, which made me think that once upon a time there must have been more gathered water there. When we later tracked down an ancient map we saw that there had indeed been various ponds that over time, presumably to intensify productivity, had been filled in. We figured we could reinstate a couple, which would firstly help the boggy fields and secondly start to attract a whole new load of wildlife.

This was the beginning of us learning how we could slowly rebuild and restore the farm in its entirety. We started on a mission to work 'with' nature on our piece of land we were caretaking for a few decades and aim to leave it in a much better state than when we took it on. Lastly, having ponds would be a lot less maintenance, more fun and cheaper than putting in a swimming pool, and in so many ways it would give our children a taste of the childhood I'd had, as well as giving Graham and I something to entertain ourselves and childish friends with.

So when we moved in – whilst we were in the original

farmhouse – the very first thing we did was to start digging the first of our two ponds. We moved in at the end of a summer, but by the next summer we had a pond complete with jetty to jump off. It was used and used and used. We invited new friends over to feast in the garden looking over the pond and spent many happy Sundays with roast meat of some sort washed down with plenty of rosé wine. On days like this, there was invariably a moment when most people would get up and wander across the field to the pond for a cool-down dip.

Pond Number Two and the stray duck that has become my alarm clock

We had dug the footings for the house itself in the depths of winter, but as soon as things started to dry out we started on the second main pond, which was by the new house. It was carefully planned because we wanted to ensure that it not only drained the whole field to avoid it being like an unusable bog for nine months of the year, but that the position was just right.

The aim was that once dug, the pond would have views across it from the kitchen and the sun would set behind it so it would reflect in the water. Well, if you're going to build a house you might as well get the compass right!!

The pond is an absolute joy.

In my book there are a few things that there is simply

not one tiny downside to. They are daffodils, honey and our pond.

Even the cup-half-emptiest person in the world would struggle to find anything but joy in these things and the pond is definitely competing for top place.

There has never been a moment where I have regretted digging it – whether it's humans swimming, inventing things that float and testing them out, or other wildlife or horticulture enjoying the mixture of sun and water that are the vitamins that nourish all living things – it is a privilege to live next to, watch and enjoy.

In fact, there is one stray wild duck who, obviously agreeing with me, has just arrived – it does a lot of quacking about half past five every morning! So far I haven't prised myself out of bed to grab the binoculars and work out where it lives and what sort of duck it is, but it's a much better and more welcome start to the day than any alarm clock.

Very excitingly I think it might have found a partner as this morning after the usual ten minutes of quacking, it was joined by a different tone of quacking. Presumably this is some form of duck dating, which I'm fully supportive of!

I'd quite like them to hang around all day so we could see them more but then being as elusive as they are hopefully keeps them out of the jaws of foxes. We did have some incubated ducks but they only lasted eighteen months before they became a fox snack, and I have become quite disheartened by the fact of life in the country that you have to clearly define 'caged pet' (i.e. alive) or 'fully free range' (i.e. fox food).

This year we will let nature bring its own wildlife to the pond instead and see how that plays out.

How to dig your own pond

When you dig a pond it can be a bit hit and miss. We had a truly lovely contractor called Metford who did our groundworks and who we worked closely together with.

First you get digging and see what the ground is made of – most of our land is thick, sticky clay, though, which is perfect. If it had been chalk, it would have been more complicated as chalk doesn't hold water very well!

Then you scrape off the topsoil, which is about a foot deep and is made from rotting-down leaves etc. – it's generally what we all think of as soil. This layer needs to be kept separate from the layers below, so you place it in a big pile to allow all the grass, weeds and roots to rot down within it.

The next layer down is the clay. Dumper truck after dumper truck was used to transport all the contents of the hole to the far end of the farm to put it along the inside of a hedge that ran along the side of the main road.

We probably made the hole a bit deeper than we might have a few years ago when the boys were little, but I knew if people were going to dive in, a few extra feet would be safer.

Finally we got down to the depth I thought least dangerous, which was about fifteen feet.

You then need to work quickly before any rain comes and starts to fill it up. We pushed in used telegraph poles as the stands for a jetty that you would be able to jump off into the middle of the pond – just like the previous pond we dug – along with an old ladder that was strapped to the side meaning you could get in and out without wading through the mud at the side. (In truth my brother did this first in his pond so I was copying him!)

Then we dug a little trench across the bottom of the pond to put in an armoured cable so we could have power to another telegraph pole where we planned to fit a fountain.

Then the bottom of the pond was 'tracked in', which effectively means it is run over with the tracks on the diggers, to try to pack down the base to stop it from leaking.

Unfortunately we did hit a seam of rock that had to be dug out as this would have let the water out of the pond, then the clay was brought back from the far pile to push into the resulting hole to get it watertight – again that was all tracked in.

The design of the pond was largely based on a 'go that far and then let's discuss' method. It's by far the most enjoyable way to create anything in my opinion.

Anyway, we got the second pond finished before the autumn and then had the joy of sitting back and watching it fill up. We fitted land drains around the new house and all those channelled down into the pond too.

The next spring, we built an 'outlet', which effectively is a small wall with a series of waterfalls that acts like the overflow of a bath so that when it rains a really massive amount, the water first collects in our pond and then only the last bit is channelled back into the ditch. Further downstream we have made various blockages called woody dams that slow down the rush of water from sudden rainfall, meaning there are lots of little areas that occasionally flood in the wood.

We have more plans of how to make the rain bend to our will so that we can enjoy the water for the time it is with us until it moves on downstream. A combination of solar-powered pumps and waterfalls circulating the water to keep it oxygenated will not only sound and look great, but also keep the water in tip-top condition for all its new inhabitants of horticulture and wildlife to enjoy.

22

My favourite room

My favourite room in the house varies from day to day. The TV room, which Graham designed so painstakingly for me and that I now use as my office, is definitely one of them. When I am working here, as I am now, I look out at the views over the pond – I can't begin to tell you how perfect it is.

Sitting here, I think about the amount we have stuffed into our lives: the desk I sit at that Graham and I bought thirty years ago in an auction; the computer with the 120,000 photos of our four sons and joyous extended family and friends waiting to be edited. The room itself so carefully planned by the man I met when he was a boy and who I am so lucky to have shared thirty rollercoaster years with. An amazing journey that has brought me here.

If you had asked either of us all that time ago how life would pan out, I most certainly wouldn't have thought it would be as wonderful as this. I know that I am so, so lucky.

But there are other favourite rooms too. I actually LOVE our bedroom partly because you can see the drive from my bed, and I love watching the comings and goings of who is arriving and leaving.

I also LOVE the kitchen, especially in the summer when you can open the bi-folding doors and watch the wildlife dancing on the pond as the sun sets across it.

Then there is the dining room, the perfect setting for dinner parties and family gatherings, and the library, which is stuffed full of all the books I plan to one day read.

The top landing has a dusty-pink, soft, squishy carpet that your feet sink into, with bookcases all around. These shelves are filled with the books that may not look as beautiful as the ones in the library downstairs but the contents of which I have largely actually read at some point in my life. Another favourite of mine is the utility/boot room, a room where Graham's and my joint dreams of organisation really culminated.

In our home in London, he suggested this plan: a cupboard for each of the children with cubby-holes to slide in their shoes, trainers and wellies and a rail and hooks for coats and school bags with each door carefully emblazoned with their name. I had a slightly alternative dream of having one large drawer with all the gloves in, one large drawer with all the hats in, etc. Graham ploughed ahead with his idea and boy, did it work.

It turns out that schools – and Graham! – have realised

that if you take ownership of your items and your space, there is slightly more chance of you:

a) Continuing to be united with them, but also
b) You might take enough ownership to actually want to put your things in your cupboard.

So down in Somerset we literally recreated the same. However this time the children were all about ten years older than the last iteration. Sadly it hasn't been the same success, perhaps it's the fact that Graham and I also have our own cupboards (reeling from the success of the last time we had done this). It might be that it worked better for city living than on a farm, where there are many different doors to leave shoes and wellies at. Our sons also have bigger bedrooms to house their belongings in.

Or perhaps we just aren't able to control our sons' lives in the same way, now they are that much older.

The extra belongings that come with country living definitely don't help. Between the beekeeping equipment, wetsuits, fluorescent building coats, waders and other outdoor countryside gear, it's just possible that our ordered London lives have been diluted away. Whatever the reason, this is not the room of dreams it once was.

Nevertheless, the doors have our names on and in the middle there is a sink for washing dirty shoes or cat bowls. It has a 'laundry maid', which is a wooden drying rack on a pulley that comes down from the ceiling, and a plug-in wall-mounted electric shoe drying rack, which is a genius piece of equipment that I discovered from my lovely friend Vic.

The technical bit

Whilst it may not look glamorous, in many ways the most impressive room in the house is the plant room (a room that has all the engineering for the house – think of the engine room in a ship).

Hour after hour of thought went into this room. If you start from scratch there is really no excuse not to get a plant room perfect. We had an impressive plant room in Rise Hall that looked and felt like you were in the bowels of a ship, but of course now we have a smaller house and so it is a smaller plant room.

Even so, I wanted it to be the 'right' engineering. 'Right' to me meant ideally at some point we would be able to have no bills as well as no requirement for the planet to be affected by the running of our home.

But we also wanted to somehow see if we could achieve being able to live in a house doing this but without compromise. Namely with as much warmth and as much hot and cold running water as we wanted.

I was convinced that if you really understood the options and put the puzzle together right, you could achieve this.

Certainly, it was one of our biggest challenges because if you don't get services right at the outset, it is complicated and expensive to buy and retrofit.

Also, it seemed absurd to be building a home from scratch and not be able to achieve this. I am not 100 per cent sure we have everything spot on yet in terms of engineering, but I am pretty certain most of the decisions that we have made were the right ones so far.

We used electric underfloor heating mats in the bathrooms, so they could be turned on or off independently of any other heating. One of the biggest problems in a larger home can be that it is tricky and expensive to isolate heating in different areas.

We had open fires in the hallway, dining room, library and sitting room and so needed the right ventilation beneath the floor with vents to the outside all in the right places to ensure they all drew really well.

At Rise Hall, engineering norms at the time meant fires were built so they easily heated a room. We wanted the same – so that with just a couple of logs, which would be easy to light, the fires would throw masses of heat into the room.

Heating itself was tricky to decide on as the build method, which was Nudura ICF (Insulated Concrete Forms), meant that theoretically we wouldn't really need heating at all.

The idea with this system is that any heat generated would be super efficiently retained inside the building due a massive amount of thermal mass, massive levels of insulation and no cold bridging. Unless you opened a window it would retain almost all of its heat, so it was hard to correctly specify the heating requirements.

I have also learnt over the years that most 'targets' and 'systems to qualify targets' are designed by people who seem to have never considered that human beings may have differing habits to those who were in this original 'thinktank'.

So let's start with the basics – many of the current solutions are based on the pre-supposition that you sleep with the window shut at night. If you don't, then you actually need an altogether different solution.

Then there is the 'heat your body not the whole house' theory of heating that only some people subscribe to. So when it's cold you layer up with a vest and jumper. If you then sit down doing nothing and are really cold you can warm up from radiant heat from a single heat source.

In our new house this would be an open fire (though obviously they wouldn't all be lit unless we have a houseful at Christmas or for a party) or our amazing Everhot electric range cooker in the kitchen (run from the solar panels on the roof), which you can stand next to or sit on top of.

This means we can open windows at night, even if it's snowing, which we like to do for fresh air. In the morning you shut the window and open the bathroom door where it is warm from the electric underfloor heating. Not only can you get dressed in there where it's toasty, but when you open the door the heat radiates out very quickly, taking the chill off the bedroom from having the window open overnight. We don't really use any other heating. The window open/shut difference is the key.

I did a survey once (not an official one but I just asked everyone I met for a few weeks!) after I suddenly realised this misassumption about 'other people' and discovered people fall into two camps: those who open windows at night 365 days a year and those who don't – and both assume everyone is the same as them!

What we in the open window camp need is to be able to react to the house being cold if, say Granny suddenly pops over for lunch or someone leaves all the doors open. We wanted to be able to raise the temperature a lot very quickly, albeit very rarely.

The air source heat pump – which we have fitted as it was required to hit current targets – is, in my opinion, not a suitable solution for heating a home if you live in this way, and the snag is if you live in this way you are unlikely to change.

It works at its best with water-based underfloor heating – it is complex and expensive in terms of space and equipment to have many different zones and would be nigh on impossible to have a zone per room. Also, as these pipes are not as hot as traditional radiators, the principle is that you take a long time to reach a pleasant heat and you hold it there. Recovery is slow, and you should keep the building sealed up to avoid the temperature dropping.

Then, with the building sealed up, you electrically or mechanically ventilate, i.e. circulate the air to avoid suffocation. It's the mechanical alternative to the opening-the-window method of the past, and avoids the room temperature dropping. This is how most modern high-rise blocks of offices, hotels or indeed apartments are heated, which is why the windows don't open.

It is logical but only if you are going to *live* to its methods. The theory being that you can walk around in your pants when it's snowing outside and have a constant temperature inside, because the building is hermetically sealed so that you don't lose temperature and ideally rarely open an exterior door. It also requires a brilliantly insulated structure with no drafts at all though (in any old building this is very tricky indeed).

I could bore for England on this subject but for us a water underfloor heating system (being the perfect dance partner for the air source heat pump) was never going to be a viable option.

An air source heat pump absorbs the heat from the air and puts this into a liquid. It runs through a heat exchanger, which gets a bit techy, but effectively it gets the liquid to about fifty-five degrees Celsius, and this then runs around in pipes under your floor.

The problem here is that at fifty-five degrees, the only

way to recover the heat if you leave a door open whilst you pack the car or open the window at night is to send the system into overdrive for a protracted period whilst it tries to recover the temperature. As it's powered by electricity, which is the most expensive power, it starts to get very pricey indeed and could take a day or two to recover anyway.

Electricity may be the greenest energy to produce theoretically, but we haven't been making enough of it in a green way in the UK by a long shot to make all that was required *before* this electric push – so a large amount of our electricity is made by burning fossil fuels. In short the national grid is in gridlock as it is – we need to *reduce* our requirement from the grid. So we fitted many dozens of solar panels to negate our electricity requirements, but even then the recovery time was still never going to work with our way of living.

In short, an air source heat pump is fine for helping us to heat the hot water (as it sits in superbly insulated tanks until you use it) but it just couldn't react how we needed it to. So we fitted a back-up oil boiler as oil is able to achieve high temperatures fast but also because I am convinced that hydrogen will be a big player in the solution to generating green energy in the future. It will be a relatively straightforward exercise as and when hydrogen can be used in domestic boilers to switch the part in our oil boiler to enable it to use hydrogen. Whilst we don't really use the oil boiler, knowing that it's there on the rare occasion we need fast heating enables the house to work as well as you could want.

Our plant room reflects many hours of theoretical work and calculations to tick the right boxes for government targets, but also to achieve what we wanted to achieve – which is a house that doesn't need much energy to run and the energy it does need can as much as possible be made from the land around it wherever possible. We also wanted to see if we could do this without compromising on how we already live.

That is a journey I am proud to say that we get closer to every year, as we tweak one system or another and balance the power we can create with the usage and settings. So far though, we have sewerage off-grid – tick, water in off-grid – nearly tick, lighting off-grid – tick, hot water off-grid – tick and heating off-grid – also nearly tick.

It is a slow burn – until we have a whole twelve months of data we won't be sure that this cocktail of solutions has taken us to where we want to be: to make this house a blueprint for how a new house like this could and perhaps should be engineered.

23

Magnolia, medlar and Christmas trees

So we now have the perfect pond and the home of our dreams, which sits in a field of about eight acres that used to contain only sheep. It has a newly tarmacked drive, which we had to do because the cost of replacing car tyres from the potholes was starting to mount up and it was cheaper long term to just 'do' the drive properly.

I keep thinking of all the outside projects I have yet to start. I am yet to build my ultimate composting system. I have a vision of a three bucketed rotational system where you have one chamber that you are filling, one rotting and one you are using, but it's still on my to-do list. I am also yet to build a small boathouse to stop our little rowing boat filling up every time it rains.

Graham and I talk endlessly about all the things on our to-do list. We talk about football goalposts that are a bit more permanent than a couple of jumpers or garden chairs. We chat about a tennis court, although I worry it will cost a fortune and won't be used enough. We talk about some outbuildings in which to put the mower and other garden machinery, but we aren't quite sure where they would be yet.

We chat about some sheds to store the bins in and I even have a cunning plan to have a small outdoor cupboard with a tap and external socket in it to house the jet washer so it is permanently plugged in, as every time I want to use it I can never find it or its various attachments.

We talk about a small shed on wheels, which I have a design for in my head, that would contain all garden games, meaning you can pull it around the garden and the badminton/football/croquet stuff is where you want it and can be put away out of the rain easily. Like everything else here, it's not actually built yet but it's definitely in the planning stages!

We chat about the to-do list like we used to about the 'dream home' that I didn't think we'd ever build. There is no urgency for this to-do list – it is just some of the stuff that happens to be on mine.

Some thoughts on to-do lists

I think there are two types of people: the to-do lister and . . .

The not to-do lister.

Life is about time – and that time has to be filled one

way or another, even if it's just sitting in a chair. What we do and the manner in which we do those things is the only difference. The to-do list might be a way of fitting more things in or just a way of sorting the things you do.

I am a to-do lister.

The trouble with a to-do lister, I now realise, is that the list is NEVER EVER empty. It's more of a mantra for life – although not as good as my main mantra, which is 'Positive Things Happen to Positive People', which, whilst my husband has always found it slightly irritating, he admits now he is older and wiser that it's just an undeniable fact of life.

Graham and I often talk about the 'why' people and the 'why not' people – or the people who 'make' problems rather than 'solve' problems – and I have come to the conclusion that the to-do list is really no more than a mental attitude thinly disguised merely as an organisational tool, it runs much deeper. It's for the person who can't just 'be'. It's for the person who can't sit still. It's more a principle that a load of things would be better if they were done.

There is an element of efficiency though – if your goal is just to fill time then you must lose all lists, whether they are shopping or reminder lists. This way fewer things can fill more time. If you want to fit more things into your life, it won't necessarily be more enjoyable but a good place to start is the to-do list, to be more efficient with brain space and time.

But what does efficiency actually *mean*? And, more importantly, what does efficiency actually achieve? It's a buzzword that has taken me most of my life to actually stand back from and think about properly. Children don't think about efficiency – they just think about today. As I got older, like a child in a sweet shop I found it impossible to resist the abundant array of possibilities out there and the temptation to say 'yes' to anything and everything was too great to turn down. The more you say yes, the more opportunities come and, perhaps born from a deep-seated fear of the fact that life is finite and might not go on as long as you think, I just stuffed more in until the only possible way of juggling all the plates was a kind of list system that in itself was totally out of control.

Which got me to thinking. If you have ever tried to clear your inbox, there is a trick. Don't start at the top, start at the bottom – you'll find that the majority of emails at the bottom of your inbox have somewhat amazingly resolved themselves by the time you get to them and can be deleted. Most of the things we worry about just sort of resolve themselves if you leave it long enough – the odd thing clearly is a bit of a disaster but even disasters resolve themselves one way or another. Which is a bit of a metaphor for life, I reckon. Half the stuff we worry about and reasons we find to stress about it are actually totally counterproductive, especially if you are stressing about doing something that is technically dressed up as something you are *meant* to be enjoying.

Here is my list of pointless things to get stressed about:

- Christmas
- Holidays
- Parties
- Going to the pub
- Going out to supper
- Meeting friends
- Talking to people on the phone.

Things it's also pointless to get stressed about because you can't do anything about them:

- The future
- The weather
- Most things in the news
- Possible future health concerns that haven't happened but most especially death.

Then that leaves OK things to get stressed about – they are things that are happening now *and* that you are able to affect, but even those leave the option of 'getting stressed' as pretty pointless. Life is a series of choices. We ALWAYS have a choice. You choose one path or another, each one having its own set of consequences. It is the consequences we need to focus on when making a choice.

Getting stressed about any of it is utterly pointless. Right now, you could eat a doughnut. You can choose: you eat it and it gives you one consequence or you don't and it gives you another. A doughnut might seem a light-hearted example, but it works for all decisions big and small. You can even not get out of bed and not go to work. It is still a choice – turning up where you are expected just has different consequences to not turning up. Never ever think you don't have a choice and never ever forget to ensure you have made that choice based on the consequences of your actions. Then you will be happy and will not be stressed.

Somehow, I have subconsciously just turned the previous paragraphs into a series of lists?! OK, I am a clearly obsessive list-writer – perhaps it comes in the same character lottery bucket as control freak – but I now realise that it's often the process of writing the list that is the calming influence rather than actually doing anything. In fact, often writing a to-do list and then losing it is just as effective – you will remember the really important things and the things you don't remember weren't actually as important as you thought they were. And much like your inbox – when you find the list at the bottom of a pile somewhere most of the things will have been done anyway or no longer need doing.

My point is you'll fill the list if it's a list you want or

need. Doing everything on it will just mean you will find more things to add that are less important. So whether your list looks like this:

- Finding the cure to cancer
- World peace
- Saving the planet
- Sorting out UK politics.

Or this:

- Worming the cat
- De-weeding the patio
- Putting the washing on
- Ringing your mum
- Getting a birthday card for a god-child AND posting it.

You're going to fill it up with this and that.

There will always be something else. My to-do lists are a major part of my life; they enable me to juggle entirely unrelated things and generally keep the plates spinning without letting too many fall and smash. I am often asked how to juggle work, a large family, etc. – I think if you wake up every morning and think, *Who am I going to disappoint today?*, then it's a pretty good baseline! But a list also helps!

Efficiency runs through a to-do lister's veins and

whilst I know I should slow down, it helps me run at a thousand miles an hour. There are lots of downsides but some of this efficiency makes life easier. As I keep telling my children, you need to be the sort of person that can be trusted with an item on someone's to-do list. Ultimately, it's about responsibility. You can only ask someone to do something on your list if they will take responsibility for it – if they can't be trusted then instead of taking something off your list, you're actually adding an extra item: to remember to ask the person if they have done the task you asked them to do, and you *still* have to do it if it hasn't been done as well.

The honest truth is if you are someone who doesn't take responsibility for things, you will end up just not being asked – as it's actually more work for people to remember to ask you if you in turn have remembered to do it and nag you to do it than it is to do it themselves. Whilst this might sound brilliant because you'll be asked to do fewer boring things, you will also be asked to do fewer interesting things and miss out on all the experiences and opportunities that get chucked in along the way. Sadly, you can't pick and choose and only do the things which sound appealing – you'll just not be asked to do anything. With a reputation for not being able to be trusted to just complete things, you'll be asked to do less and less.

Weirdly, if you can finish a very simple task to completion – i.e. take the bins out AND put a new bin liner in AND pick up the random escaped bit of rubbish floating around the garden AND not walk over something on the stairs that is heading upstairs – life will just lay more in your lap. You are a rare commodity and opportunity will head your way, whereas the 'get out of it by doing it badly or not at all' attitude will indeed mean you don't have to take the bins out and will mean you have to deal with being shouted at. BUT it also will mean you will not be the first person to be asked when someone is missing a driver to get a sports car from A to B, or who needs help organising a festival or getting a leading sports team to the Olympic stadium. Ultimately the 'why not' rather than the 'why' person will have more opportunity and have more fun – they will be 'luckier', but they will have made their own luck.

The to-do list enables the ultimate juggle, and the fitness you develop in your mind enables you to be nimble and agile of thought. I overheard a conversation an elderly gentleman was having the other day whilst I was in a doctor's waiting room. He was explaining that he would be having Christmas Day on his own again this year – as he did every year. I nearly leapt out of my chair and invited him to Christmas lunch with us and my extended family, who would have been somewhat surprised at the new addition to the day but would have rolled with it in their own brilliant way.

But then this gentleman was asked the more obvious question – did he not have any friends? Yes, he explained, but they don't eat until 3 p.m. and that was too late for him as he'd be hungry. Out went my invite – as from past experience of hosting many Christmases for between eighteen and sixty people – I couldn't honestly say when lunch would be eaten apart from sometime between 1 p.m. and 8 p.m. (Though one year I put the turkey in the wrong Aga oven and it was ready at 7 a.m.! By four in the afternoon, when we ate it, the gravy acted more like glue to stick the desiccated turkey loosely together. It made no difference to the day – apart from adding a story to tell which was much more interesting than 'we had a really nice lunch'.)

I realised that the inflexibility of this elderly gentleman was what kept him at home, doubtless cooking his small chicken, potatoes and sprouts for one. Or perhaps he is so happy with his own company that he keeps the inflexibility the way it is to ensure that he doesn't have to share the day with friends or relatives. Either way, I felt reassured that it was a choice. He didn't seem unhappy with his choice and the fact that it wouldn't have been my choice, as I'd rather starve than spend Christmas on my own, just makes the rich tapestry of life and the different people in it more interesting and exciting.

***

I do accept though that there are many, many things that have made it off my to-do list and now are on the 'actually done' list. Though as I said before, I'll always find more things to do.

Around two sides of the house we put down gravel, in which we dug planting pockets and filled them with soil in order to have good beds for plants to grow up the walls. These, needless to say, have still to be planted. The other two sides of the house have hardstanding, where we built up the levels with hardcore (lumps of gravel and stone) and topped it with a crushed limestone rather than paving. It is fabulous in many ways because its organic and moves around and drains brilliantly but is a tiny bit annoying (as I said to Graham it would be!).

This is because the dust from it tends to be walked into the house. But it's only a tiny bit annoying rather than very annoying, largely because I've decided I don't care if we have a super clean and tidy house. It's why we built the house in the style it is, which is sometimes kindly called 'faded grandeur' or 'shabby chic'!

Behind the pond we've planted a variety of trees that, in time, will grow to be a verdant multicoloured array of gorgeousness.

As for the rest of the garden, I must admit it is a tiny bit overwhelming. Where to start with a massive empty field? It's hard to know where to begin. It's a bit like having agoraphobia with so much space.

Bit by bit, we make a plan – like a treehouse and a

greenhouse, although they would need to be considerably bigger to make much of a dent in the field. We
built a very brilliant chicken run (well, actually it was
originally for turkeys but the turkeys were eaten for
Christmas, so now we have our rescue chickens in it so
we can have eggs).

It's the spaces in between that still lie empty and a
little barren. Even the few hundred trees and shrubs
planted in this field don't really make much of a dent
in it yet as they will take a good ten to fifteen years to
really come into their own.

Clearly this is a very first-world problem. I am hardly
expecting much sympathy with 'my garden is too big so
where do I start' problems but nevertheless that's where
we are.

I think with gardens the key is to close down the space
into 'rooms', much as you would with a house, which
always looks bigger and more interesting once you put
up walls. You then need the furniture inside a home,
but plants and trees in a garden to furnish these 'rooms'.

But theories are easier than practice, especially as even
once you have an idea of the views you want to create
you then have to choose exactly which plants and trees
to buy, and even then you have to end up buying the
plants and trees that are actually available and affordable rather than the ones you might like.

We did try and close down the view by putting one
of the shipping containers where we might have built

a wall to see what it would be like, but quickly moved it as it meant that when you drove down the drive you couldn't see the pond and sunset. We went back to scratching our heads.

I have always slightly dreamt of a walled garden and in terms of future-proofing the garden, I think with a pond it would be wise to slowly plan a closed-off area outside the kitchen for future tiny children or puppies to be contained. But again that would close off the view of the pond to a certain degree.

The view versus cosy garden spaces debate continues.

We are lucky enough to have unusual and specialist trees that have been given to us along the way by lovely friends and family, and each time we debate where they should go in the open-plan nothingness. Tree by tree, they have to go somewhere so in so many ways that really helps!

Our latest gifted tree is a magnolia. Magnolia are marvellous trees and we luckily have several already – the 'where to put it' discussions are currently in full flow.

I also have a really gorgeous rare tree that I was given for my birthday by a good friend. The tree is called a medlar (the fruit of which for 900 years was somewhat crudely called 'open-arse' but people still ate it!). We also have the Christmas tree from this year, which I got with roots on, and we need to plant out in the hope it makes it.

These 'planting decisions' seem to take up a great deal

of time and effort and we do a bit of going around in circles, largely because we don't fully agree on what is to go where.

We have a steep bank I can see when I sit up in bed and drink tea and, one day, fed up with all this indecision, I got a massive bag of wildflower seed and chucked it on. Typically, we then had an unexpected freeze two days later so I didn't hold my breath – but even these are now all peeping through.

Last March I did the same thing, throwing a load of wildflower seeds instead of grass seed around the outlet from the pond to stop where it overflowed ending up a big muddy patch that eventually would have been washed away.

Boy, did that deliver – from March to November we had flower after flower popping up – it was the gift that kept on giving and I am thoroughly excited to see them arriving again this year.

Wildflower seeds prefer really poor soil with stones, and then they over time compost themselves down and fix the soil by covering it in a rich layer of composted material.

It's nature's very clever way of fixing soil and not only is it visually joyous, but it is also a delightful gift to my bees and the insects above and beneath the soil that benefit too.

Since moving to Somerset, I think I appreciate plants and flowers and the crossover between the two more. So I am planting a lot of shrubs and trees for 'cutting'.

It will be a few years before they are really bearing fruit but if you put a bit of thought into your planting, you can have joyous things to bring inside to blend the inside and outside of your home together.

I look back now to when we lived with just a tiny little balcony thirty years ago and realise if I'd thought about it a bit more and put a bit more time into it, I could have had a tiny piece of overgrown gorgeousness. But then when I was young, I was much more interested in things I could change overnight. You stay up all night and work really hard, and at the end of it you had a room that looked completely different.

With a garden you need patience, but then as you get older the years pass more quickly and so the joy of being able to transform an interior space is a little tarnished by how quickly it needs touching up or things need fixing.

Whereas by the time you catch your breath – a good two years later for the middle-aged me – the garden is just thinking about doing as you hoped.

I was awake in the night a few weeks ago and, although it is a very silly time to go shopping, I found myself buying a few thousand bulbs that were on special offer.

I was spurred on by 'finding' a bluebell wood on the farm during lockdown, which I'd missed the first year we moved in by just being too busy to happen to walk there.

I guilted the children into helping and we just about managed to get all my new bulbs in the soil. Now it is spring, the fruits of our labour have popped out to reward us – so, so worth it!

I have also bought a special thistle digging-out fork, which is genius as it removes the root (well, actually I bought two, thinking it was a job that looked more fun with company). Again, this needs patience but it also needs you to accept you cannot tame nature to your will without manpower of an infinite kind. I have come to the conclusion that I don't want to tame nature; I just want to trim it around the edges.

It is the maverick nature of nature that is one of its greatest joys. It does as it chooses – it will allow you to come along for the ride and piggy-back on its skills, but work against them at your peril.

I have no doubt that things will not be as we are currently planning; so in a few years' time the update of this chapter will bear no relation to what I currently envisage. But, tree by tree and plant by plant, we will build on what we have.

Increasingly, I find myself talking about cuttings with friends and have started to ask for seeds for my birthday – so clearly either age or the task of creating the garden is taking over, just like how cigarettes and a lighter in your pocket in your youth are replaced by dental floss and Gaviscon when you get older.

24

Building the treehouse of my childhood dreams

A treehouse is a bit like a sports car or a St Bernard dog. The trouble with a sports car is that if you drive one when you are young, everyone knows you are a massively overindulged child who has been bought a sports car you didn't deserve by parents who have spoilt you.

On the other hand, if you drive a sports car when you *can* afford one, then you are too old to drive a sports car and look like you are rather pathetically trying to relive your youth.

Both looks are not good and to kid yourself you drive a sports car for any reason other than what other people think is just a big fat lie because we all know it isn't the easiest or most comfortable or most affordable way to get from A to B.

Similarly, a St Bernard dog at its best is like a MASSIVE, giant, warm, walking teddy bear. As you know I spent most of my childhood wanting one of these dogs and yet when I left home I never got one. At any point in those years I *could* have got the dog of my dreams – but haven't.

Why? Because even at the tender age of seventeen, the poo that would come out of a dog that size and the smelliness of that amount of fur if unpreened overwhelmingly won the argument.

My son has taken up the mantle and tries all possible tactics to persuade me to get one of these dogs. But I've been a mother for long enough to know that I wouldn't be getting a 'family' dog – I would be getting myself a dog and your child would 'borrow' it now and then to play with, whilst I would have to deal with all the nasty bits.

Which to be honest is exactly what happened with all the other caged pets, such as guinea pigs, rabbits, gerbils, etc., which is why we don't have them anymore.

So, just like a sports car or a dog, all children want a treehouse – well, I know I desperately wanted one. Much of my childhood was spent turning bits of garden sheds into little dens.

My brother and I even dug holes in the ground as 'bunkers', though these were often not as deep as we had originally planned as they were very hard work to dig and we generally started them in the height of summer. They also filled up with water as soon as it rained, rendering them fairly unusable.

A child, though, usually doesn't have the ability or, to be frank, the experience, nor money or transportation for materials to build a treehouse.

They can – like I did when I was younger – gather bits of wood and nails, screw or tie them into trees and then climb the tree and sit in or under the bits of wood, but all this is a far cry from the woodland castle of my childhood dreams.

I also think that a lot of adults still secretly want a treehouse – they just can't justify building one until they have a child themselves. Then they either build one, claiming it is for the child, or insist they don't have the time or space to do so.

I went with a third option – to build one entirely to suit myself. I had dabbled with building treehouses over the years, as a child and then at Rise Hall, but now I was finally getting the chance to build the treehouse of my dreams. So luckily I had a lot of experience to draw on. We'd once bought a field to escape the chaos of building work at our house in London. There I built a cabin that was like a treehouse – but the treehouse of MY dreams for MYself. Well, actually, to be fair, Graham and the boys all played their part, but it definitely was for me – not for them.

Graham had hoped that this would be the place where I would finally relax and slow down. Able to get away from everything, this would be a place and space in which all the things I mean and want to do, like write a children's book, would come to me. It most definitely was my very, very happy place.

The honest truth is we didn't use it nearly as much as intended. We had a water supply but there was no power and it was delightfully internet free.

All that aside, we had many happy weekends there and in many ways it paved the way for the big move to the country some years later. But the grown-up me did have the treehouse of my childhood dreams, built by the grown-up me and the grown-up me's family. We set about building it with loads of insulation and some very brilliant double glazed windows that had been unwant-ed samples in weird sizes and colours, which couldn't have been better for a treehouse cabin!

It's hard when you have spent decades in the building industry not to build something well if you are going to build it at all – I also do feel that environmentally, even if you are largely using stuff that isn't wanted, it still takes some of the Earth's resources to build something and so you should build well and build to last.

So that's what we did.

Honestly, we just started. This is a truly joyous way to build. It is the precise opposite of how you build a house.

I looked at a few rooms I liked being in and measured how big they were. Then I figured a balcony would be good to sit on outside and that I might as well have a walkway all around the cabin, so added a few feet here and there.

Then we literally stuck in a few posts, cantilevered a few fixings off a tree until we had a good sturdy deck the size planned – and that was pretty much that.

The steps were made from bits of wood leftover from various sites we had running and bolted together, and the banister around the deck was made from trees lying around.

Then we just built stud walls out of sections of 4" x 2" timber also leftover – the walls were the height of the timbers because, quite simply, that was the timber we had.

We used leftover insulation to fill in the stud walls and clad the inside with offcuts of ply.

We bought some cladding for the outside, which was a rough sawn log (it's called wavy edge as it still has the bark edge showing).

All in all it was a building that sort of evolved from things we already had.

The final piece of the puzzle was to lay a floor which came from a load of parquet squares that must have been ripped out of some building at some point and were covered in bits of chicken poo.

We found this at a farmyard in Norfolk where we had gone to collect a fire surround that they were selling but the parquet caught my eye. There wasn't enough for a proper room and I wasn't quite sure if we'd ever use it, so I didn't get it.

When the treehouse cabin started, I got back in touch

and unsurprisingly the parquet was still there – £100 later I was driving away with the panels, which were then fitted on the floor.

It's interesting to me that this is how a building would have been built in the past, and indeed in many countries still would be. It is utterly organic and utterly logical, and there is something entirely liberating about building as you go along rather than drawing something, planning something and rigidly sticking to the plan.

For me it was the antidote to the building we did in our daily lives. The treehouse cabin had no deadline and no formal plan. It ended up about ten-foot square, which is just the perfect amount of space to get away for a very enjoyable moment of peace but also as a family to spend time together away from the city.

When we finally moved to Somerset and were no longer city-based, we hardly visited our little hideaway and sold it in my bid to achieve a simpler life all in one place – but we recreated one the same at our new home.

25

The perfect greenhouse

Having a greenhouse has also always been on my bucket list. But it was when we eventually moved to Somerset that I could make this a reality. I wanted a little potting-shed type of greenhouse where I could potter around (taking up pottering being my new year's resolution), planting things, tending to them and picking things to eat.

But then my humble plans for a small seed-planting space got a bit carried away. In my defence the plans escalated for a very logical reason, namely that if you are going to build a greenhouse to go with a house that's been designed to last several hundred years, then the greenhouse should also last that long.

Also, if you are going to build something that will last that long, it needs to be of a design that will stand the test of time and look not only appropriate in its setting but also be useful to the occupiers of the house.

So we built a larger greenhouse than originally planned

and one that is really, really beautiful to look at. Honestly, it is the greenhouse of our dreams.

Over the years, Graham and I have seen a few utterly incredible orangeries on our journey around various decrepit stately homes but one in particular stands out, which we saw deep in rural Wales.

It was like walking into a greenhouse in Kew Gardens and was so big that in its day, the house must have been armed with dozens of gardeners to tend to the amount of plants it would have housed in the orangery.

But those days were long gone and, like the house, it had fallen into terrible disrepair. To have restored it would have been eye-wateringly tricky, with all the dainty timber glazing bars needing painting (if not replacing) and large numbers of the panes of glass broken. The access would have been very tricky and restoration very expensive indeed. You'd then be left with a single-glazed greenhouse; whilst Kew Gardens in south London has the benefit of endless paying visitors to fund maintenance, that would be unlikely to happen here in Wales.

But even in its neglected state, it was a thing of wonder. Although there were no plants left in it, you could see the potential for plants and it was that possibility that made it so very exciting.

The stately home itself was built of dull grey stone and had, I think, at one point been a school. Now only one slightly unusual middle-aged single lady lived there.

She was 'caretaking' the house, living in one room, surrounded by so many piles of 'things' that either the caretaking job had caused her to become a hoarder or the job was most appealing to someone who already had it as a hobby.

We didn't buy that house (perhaps not surprising as our gut feeling about the place wasn't great) but we did LOVE the orangery there.

So when I suggested a small greenhouse to Graham, we were probably always going to get carried away.

However, from what I had seen in the past I was certain our greenhouse HAD to be made of metal, not wood.

Whilst wood is pretty, there was literally zero chance that we would repaint it regularly enough for it to not deteriorate. Wood can last indefinitely if fully maintained, but if not, when the rot sets in it's only a matter of years before it would end up needing demolishing.

On the other hand, an aluminium greenhouse would arrive factory-sprayed in the colour of our choice, wouldn't need re-painting and theoretically doesn't biodegrade with rain and sun.

Which brings me onto a point about the planet. There are things that are considered 'good' or 'bad'. But it's not as straightforward as that because not all wood is good and not all plastic is bad.

What we really need to consider is trying to not 'buy' more new 'stuff'. Shopping is fun – but second-hand shopping in a charity shop, auction or car-boot sale is the same fun. It's just recycling the 'stuff' that already exists, whilst creating jobs as the 'stuff' is circulated – so in my mind it's entirely fine.

Just as we built the house out of concrete and had UPVC windows *because* they don't biodegrade, I believe that the right choice for a greenhouse is aluminium and not wood for the same reason.

Our greenhouse should be standing (assuming the football/golf/croquet balls don't get it first) in a hundred-plus years – so we had to get it right.

So I knew what materials we wanted to use, then it was just a question of the design. We found a great company called the Greenhouse People and together we pooled all our knowledge.

We learnt from various greenhouses we have come across, not just the one in Wales but also a rather wonderful Victorian conservatory that some great friends of ours own. We have welcomed in many a new year there, wrapped up in hats and gloves against the cold. In summer, too, we have spent many evenings in there under their bountiful dripping grapes.

Like theirs, we decided to make our greenhouse a bit more 'solid' so had dwarf walls built around the perimeter using the leftover stone from the house. These are walls that are about a foot high, which the greenhouse then sits on. Through these walls, in four places just before the top, we cut the stone and put a small length of flexible four-inch pipe through the wall. This meant we could plant the roots of grape vines outside and then feed them through these pipes to get to the inside, where the leaves and fruit flourish in the warmer protected environment.

The beauty of this is, with the roots outside there is no danger that, once established, they will need watering.

I also planted a passion flower through one of the holes as I don't seem to be able to get over how utterly beautiful the flowers are and, as if ordered from Mother Nature herself, this passion flower, which only went in a year ago, has flowered month after month. I never tire of staring at its purple, white, yellow and black tiny handfuls of perfection.

As to size, our greenhouse has ended up being about twenty-four feet long and ten feet wide, with shelving down the sides to put plants on.

This has meant that I can grow enough salad to feed us all and guests for nine months of the year. It's a step closer to my dream of self-sufficiency – something that perhaps had its seeds planted by my parents in my youth. (Although when I look at the French bean plants' output it makes each bean more valuable than caviar in terms of time spent nurturing them!)

Once built, I put my Roberts Radio in there, largely because the Roberts Radio is one of my favourite possessions. I love it for two reasons. Firstly, my mother had a brown one that she always listened to and secondly because it is a single-use item, and I LOVE a single-use item because you don't get distracted by all the other stuff on a phone or laptop. I begrudge the fact that to listen to music on my phone I have to be in the same place as all my work is – it's like having to stay in the office nonstop 24/7.

Ideally, I would also stick the rather brilliant wind-up gramophone I found in an auction in there too, but I don't think it or the records would like the massive variation in temperature and humidity. Come to think of it, I don't suppose my Roberts Radio likes it much but, happily, it seems to be surviving.

There is nothing as fine as taking a mug of tea out to the greenhouse and turning on the radio – I flit between various radio stations depending on the mood and even *Gardeners' Question Time*. Not so long ago I would have immediately turned it off but these days I get out my pencil and a piece of paper for tips!

I potter about discussing with my plants why they are or are not happy in there, tending to my various seed trays. I nip out tomatoes and replant the edible flowers and tie up my French beans.

I have also started a mean obsession with keeping the cardboard centres of loo rolls and cutting kitchen roll innards in half to use these to plant sweet peas, which may be a bit pointless as you can't eat them but are fabulously smelly and look beautiful.

I have a 'next week plan' to chop up an old bit of downpipe in the barns into foot-long sections and then tie them to the legs of my treehouse, so the sweet peas can pop out of the top to enable them to flourish and just be without being accidentally strimmed.

I honestly can't tell you how enjoyable it all is. In fact, I would go so far as to say that the greenhouse and tea are now two of my very favourite things in the world. Put them together and to my mind you have pretty much reached perfection.

We had an old sofa which was originally from Ikea and was our first 'new' sofa that we bought about thirty years ago, and that old friend too has joined me in my greenhouse along with a few old straw hats that have seen better days and any other bits and pieces I'm too sentimentally attached to discard but am not sure where they should live.

It's a happy place and I am very fortunate indeed to have so many happy memories to reflect upon in there. I enjoy it so, so much.

A greenhouse helps to ground you and centre you – a lifelong dream come true.

I am lucky indeed.

26

Three dogs, three chickens, some sheep and a cat called Alley

I've always thought you know where 'home' is by where your pets are. We did take our cat and dog up and down to Rise Hall, but our limitations on pets was largely based on what we could have in our home in London.

Now home is Somerset, I could potentially have the pygmy goat that I have dreamt of getting since the day I left home. Graham promised me one and I did think he'd have delivered on that promise by now, but in the ultimate game of dare neither of us really wants to take on the responsibility for it and so, four years later, we still don't have one.

Perhaps in time, when we have the garden better planned out and the fencing and looseboxes built for pets, we might get pygmy goats. But then there is so much else to get on with that 'pet housing' is pretty low on the to-do list.

Having said that . . . we do have a few rescue ex-battery hens – and perhaps a couple of pigs are on the cards as if we are going to eat meat, we would at least know they have had a happy life. And maybe half a dozen sheep . . . I did a lambing season in New Zealand when I was eighteen and learnt a little bit about lambing – though it turns out New Zealand lambing is considerably more 'hands off' than UK lambing, so my experience might be considered a little rudimentary here in the UK.

I am fully aware that having only six sheep means they are simply pets (that you would eat). To be farming sheep, you need around 1,000 or at least several hundred, but as sheep are obsessed with dying in any way they can I am not sure I am cut out to be a sheep farmer myself. We did have about 1,000 on the farm when we first bought it but the pleasure to pain ratio means we don't anymore.

We have considered a couple of alpacas, but again they would be pets, and without running a petting farm they would be hard work with little reward, which is why we don't have them yet. I did also consider a donkey or Shetland pony, but again the pain to pleasure ratio rings through my brain and tells me no.

That's the problem. By the time you have the freedom to get whatever pets you like, you end up not getting them because the 'looking after' is not compensated with the 'cute fluffy' factor. When I was a little girl I loved all little animals, from kittens to puppies to baby rabbits, deer, goats, sheep and ponies – you name it, I loved them and wanted them to love me. As I have got older, my appetite for small, sweet, fluffy things has remained the same although this has been tempered with the reality of how long it takes to get bored of said pet and the looking after of said pet.

But, somewhere along the line growing up, I hit on the perfect solution: a petting farm. With a petting farm you can have all the animals you fancy but you can end up paying someone else to muck them out and feed them when you can't be bothered. With visitors, they pay to come, so you don't have to go to work and earn money to pay for the animals' upkeep.

Basically, you have free pets without the work. So from about fifteen years of age, when I first came across a petting farm, it has loosely been on my bucket list of 'things I think I'd like to have'.

The only snag is that the more businesses we started up and ran, the more I realised that a business isn't as easy to run as I once thought. As well as the onerous layers of regulations, finding the right people to employ can be really tricky. I also realised that when you run a team, you end up really dealing only with the problems.

But it wasn't the problems I was very interested in, more the ideas and creativity of setting up the business in the first place.

As a result, the petting farm of my dreams still hasn't happened, even though technically we have now lived on a farm for four years where I could have started one.

The other snag with starting a business these days is that the interpretation of regulations required, even in a forward-thinking county such as Somerset, can be overwhelming.

If you wanted to have a few animals and 'see how it went', which is how many of the petting farms and dare I say it even larger safari parks such as Longleat started out, you might find the regulatory requirements very challenging.

I wonder whether even the famous Glastonbury Festival, where Graham and the boys are playing this year, would have ever got off the ground if it tried to start now. In those days it was allowed to start small; it then grew in the direction that it evolved in, taking the growing numbers of employees and businesses along with it.

'Evolve' is no longer something that is generally considered acceptable.

Having built a business in the north-east of England and having been met with a firm 'no' in terms of any support for building a business there from the local authority, I do feel that the West Country is rather keener to embrace people wanting to invest their hard-earned money and grow local opportunity.

In the West Country they seem much happier to let people spend their money on restoring buildings and farmland and investing in enterprises that employ lots of people who might otherwise have had to move away to find work or just accept they had to work in jobs that they didn't find engaging in any way.

There are two ways to regenerate an area – the carrot or the stick. The principle of this is that you remove the money from the wealthier people somewhere else in the country and then sift it through a few layers of bureaucracy, which dilutes the amount by a goodly sum, until you end up handing it out to people in an area where there is no opportunity so they can buy food and clothes.

The other way is to start businesses in the areas that appeal to people in other parts of the country who have money, so that these people choose to come and spend their money there.

As such, anything that might appeal to tourists, or businesses where people choose to buy services or products directly, is organic regeneration and makes jobs on the ground for people – and in my view should be enabled as much as humanly possible.

So theoretically, if I were to want to start a petting farm still, I honestly think I should be encouraged to do so. However, I think that ship has sailed in my life as I have reached the realisation that a 'pet' is something that costs you money and time, and you need to really love it and want it before embarking on a journey with it.

Also, with my endless belief that I should be

responsible for my own actions, I simply can't get any more pets unless I personally take responsibility for their care, and right now I am at full capacity with two dogs, four cats and six chickens.

That's not to say that over the years we haven't enjoyed our share of other pets. Whilst still living in London, we did have a couple of Gordon Ramsay's sheep once for a show he did. In the slightly crazy world of TV, the producers wanted to take the sheep around to people's lawns, grazing them before they were slaughtered and Gordon cooked and served them.

We had a pretty lovely garden and large lawn by London standards and so we got a call asking if they could fence the lawn between our flowerbeds and graze a few sheep for a couple of weeks. They promised to pay to return the lawn to perfect condition so I agreed, thinking it might be the closest we'd ever get to having the lawn of our dreams.

Also, the children were aged between two and eight at the time and I thought it would be fun for them.

The fencing and the sheep duly arrived along with a poor runner, who turned up every day to tend to the sheep and to feed them.

A couple of weeks later off they went, giving us the money to get someone to fix our lawn. Whereupon Graham bought a bag of grass seed, a couple of bags of topsoil dressing and a rake, and proceeded to just titivate the existing lawn himself. He flatly refused to use the money for the planned returf by an expert lawn company when we could have a few family jollies instead!

Without the excitement of the sheep who, by the way, were taken to the Beckham's after us, we were left with our array of rabbits, hamsters and gerbils.

I have a brilliant video of one of the gerbils in the driver's seat of the boys' remote-controlled sports car – head out of the window like it was going to go whizzing up and down the landing.

We had a few chickens at one point when I got carried away with our country-style garden in London, or perhaps I was trying in my own little way to hark back to my own childhood despite living in the city.

So we got a chicken coop that was on wheels, which we could move around the garden, enabling the grass to recover.

The truth was that the lawn, having failed to recover from sheep-gate, certainly wasn't going to recover from chicken-gate and the children being children couldn't resist letting them out.

The chickens were pretty cool actually – putting up with a considerable amount of over-loving and even bathing with the children and spending considerably more time inside our house than I had personally planned, as chickens don't seem to have any control over their lavatory activities. (I learnt recently that all birds don't poo and wee from different places; it all comes out of one hole, which is why it's so sloppy and slimy – a truly revolting yet fascinating fact for you!)

Anyway, our four pet chickens delivered eggs diligently and began to roost up various trees, which lulled me into thinking they might be happier there than in their pen and still safe from the foxes.

I was wrong.

We didn't replace the chickens after that (in London) and I gave the chicken pen to a friend. I think the propensity for foxes in urban areas is just too prolific and they are far too aggressive to want to encourage them into our garden with tasty chicken treats.

Then there are the cats.

I had a very, very adored cat called Alley, who I had for about fourteen years. He eventually had to be put down amidst an almost-breakdown from me, when the children were about two, four, six and eight. We dropped them at my brother's house, which was near us in London at the time, whilst Graham drove to the vet for 'the deed' to be done. I don't think I have cried as much about anything in my life as when my beloved Alley died.

Grief is a weird one and I think comes out in its own sweet way as and when it chooses, but looking back now Alley was my friend and I loved him and he loved me – in terms of a relationship that is about as good as it gets! Or perhaps it was such a simple relationship with no repercussions in any way, so I was able to just give into grief. We buried him with the other pets in the garden.

Alley was a 'before children' pet. I found pets different 'after children'. But we got another cat who inevitably in London ended up pregnant within nanoseconds. That cat – ingeniously named Mittens by one of the boys' friends – had her kittens in Laurie's bed when he was about a year old, much to the children's utter delight.

The kittens grew and then another set arrived before we managed to catch Mittens and have her spayed – after three litters and most of our friends locally taking a kitten, we finally got her to the vet!

I like cats – they do what they want to do. You can't own a cat – they just have staff and I should know as I spend my days tending to the needs of the four we currently have: Bogey, Pipi, Mango and Quinsten (all named by the boys but I'm hoping you'd have realised that!). Dogs, on the other hand, definitely have owners.

We got our first dog, a Miniature Dachshund called Daisy, at the same time as Laurie was born. Everyone told me that you shouldn't get a puppy at the same time as having a baby but I didn't listen – and I was wrong.

It's really hard work having both. Laurie won the emotional competition for my time and love, so Daisy, who I really also loved, was a bit brought up by my other children.

Bearing in mind they were all a bit feral anyway, they probably weren't the best role models!

She was carried around; they got in her cage and

over-cuddled her. She was put in their beds and generally mauled.

Needless to say the house-training part of her puppy-
hood didn't go so well, so she was definitely a 'kitchen
dog' as much as possible.

Sadly, just after we moved to Somerset, Daisy died
and was replaced by Maple, a Cockapoo. I wasn't going
to get another puppy so quickly but my lovely niece
Freya found some puppies and sent me the details; one
long car journey to Cornwall with Billy and Raffey later
we returned with a tiny ball of black fluff who has lit up
all our lives.

Maple in turn had four puppies (also in our bed –
there is a theme here somehow!), the runt of which we
kept – Piccolo. It is safe to say that they are much loved
by all the family. This, I have decided, is quite enough
pets for now.

Apart from bees. I have decided you can never have
enough bees.

27

How I learnt the painful way that bees are the best pets in the world

The lessons learnt from bees and the keeping of bees has been largely one of the most enjoyable and rewarding things I have done in the search for a simpler life.

This is because all you actually do is provide a lovely luxury hotel for the bees. They'll leave if they fancy it – but if they don't you can enjoy watching them flying in and out, pollinating everything that they touch (they can fly around three miles from their hive) as they co-operatively search for food to bring back and share with everyone else.

I would 100 per cent recommend that, if you can find the space, add 20,000 pets to your family in the form of a hive and colony. And I say this even as someone who has ended up in A & E after something of an angry skirmish with my clever, honey-making and, as it turns out, ferociously protective pets!

It all started innocently enough.

It was a beautiful sunny day – beekeeping days always

are, as you want to try and avoid opening the lid if it's really cold or raining as the bees have to try and warm the hive up again. Think of it like someone opening the back and front doors on a chilly day.

I generally bee-keep with one of my younger two sons and this particular day I set off very happily with Laurie in tow. My smoker was all set. These things are absolutely genius: metal tins you put strips of old cardboard in and light – they have a section on the back which is like a mini bellows and it puffs smoke out of the funnel at the top.

The smoke tricks the bees into thinking there might be a forest fire and so they go into survival mode and focus on eating as much honey as they can in preparation for abandoning the hive.

This in turn distracts them from the intruder, who they might otherwise be tempted to all aim for and sting to prevent them from threatening the colony. It is a method that has been used for centuries and is amazingly effective as part of interacting with the bees.

At this point my smoker was lit and I was using it to calm the bees down. But I had foolishly decided to bring my over-enthusiastic dog, who chose that precise moment to bounce around beside us.

Piccolo's over-enthusiastic 'friend making' with our other 20,000 pets went down about as well as it does with our elderly cat (her main defence being a sweeping clawed paw). The bees preferred certain death in this instance (they die if they sting) to rid themselves of their eager new canine friend.

The first I heard was a terrible yelp, then more yelps. I looked up from the hive to see the dog running madly in circles. By the time I got to her the poor thing was literally buzzing.

I then learnt lots more about bees. The hard way. I was top-to-bottom clad in my bee suit, but being a little mean of nature hadn't bought proper beekeeping gloves and instead had put on some gardening gloves that were tucked into my sleeves.

At least I had some protection – unlike Piccolo's long, lion-like fur, which now had masses of bees wrapped up in it. So I did what I thought best in the spur of the moment and with my right hand started squashing the trapped bees between my thumb and forefinger. It was the last thing I wanted to do but guttingly I didn't feel I had an alternative in the situation I found myself in.

By this stage I was far enough away from the hive to have some, but not too many, bees flying around us. I brushed off the ones around Piccolo's face – then picked her up and listened for where the others were trapped in her fur, and all those that I couldn't brush away I continued to squash.

Their friends were not impressed, quite reasonably, because what I realised afterwards was that bees talk to each other in their own very effective bee language.

They also send out very, very effective smell signs for other bees to read before dying to make damn certain all their colony know about it. And, much like a pub brawl with your own 'clan', rather than leaving the scene they come and get stuck in.

With bees, saving the colony comes first and staying alive comes second so stinging is high up on their solutions list. My executioner's hand may have been clad in a gardening glove but as it was designed for gardening it only had protection on the front, not the back. That side had a fabric panel presumably designed to let air in – and, as I discovered to my cost, bee stings.

So that's where they landed – on the murderous hand that had taken their family members.

By this point I had squashed about fifty bees and the dog was now nearly buzz-free. As the seconds went by, I noticed the bees were landing on me but I was prioritising Piccolo, lifting her up and listening for further trapped bees – and squashing them.

Bee stings don't hurt that much initially – that comes a bit later – and I think adrenaline probably helps when you have your much-loved dog to save and, yes, a very helpful son, but one you are also responsible for, right next to you.

The situation was also entirely of my own making and so I needed to extract us all from it as safely as possible.

Buzz-free, I sent Laurie back to the house with a very subdued Piccolo, with instructions to watch her carefully, tell Graham and take her to the vet if it looked like it was necessary.

Next, I needed to put the top back on the beehive so the remaining bees would be safe and warm, as I had by that time decided it wasn't the day for socialising with any more bees. And that's when my hand really started to hurt. And I mean *really* hurt.

The bees were still landing on my pheromone-coated hand. I could feel lots of stings starting to throb and I realised these gardening gloves were not a wise move.

I got the hive back together and walked away as quickly as possible. Bees do leave you if you go away. They don't want to die. They just want you to not kill their family and leave them alone to get on with living their lives, so they did leave me alone as I moved further away.

There were about a dozen stings on the back of my hand – but mercifully the rest of me had escaped being stung as I was better covered by my bee suit, so I didn't think much more about it.

I got back to the house, gratefully abandoned all beekeeping clothes, and figured we'd all live to fight another day. But then over the next hour or so my hand proceeded to double in size – I swallowed some antihistamines but the next morning it was even bigger. Gone was my late forties wrinkled hand and in its place was a puffy, red, blotchy one.

I resorted to A & E because the GP didn't have any appointments for a few days. At the hospital they gave me more antihistamines and antibiotics because by then the swelling was up my forearm towards my elbow. Luckily all was well a few days later.

I learnt to respect my bees more. I also invested in proper beekeeping gloves for us all. And whilst the dogs still walk to the hives with me, I would never ever open a hive again with them not being held well out of the way!

So now I am the *very* responsible owner of two hives containing two colonies. One my brother gave me (he is also a beekeeper and is the one that introduced me to beekeeping in the first place), and the other is a swarm that I collected with a dedicated veteran of beekeeping, Lionel.

Lionel is a retired local dairy farmer and has kept bees for decades. He has a long beard and is effortlessly calm, although it is hard to say which came first – the calm or the bees. What he doesn't know about bees isn't worth knowing and I was so lucky to collect a swarm with him, which was a totally amazing life experience where he taught me so, so much more about bees in general.

So this is what SHOULD happen when you lift the lid off your hive: once you have lifted off the lid, carefully place it on the ground. Below this is another board, an inner cover that gives ventilation to where the magic is going on beneath.

Beneath this board the layers start. You often need to unstick each layer as the bees have done a great job of filling all the holes and cracks with propolis to exclude the drafts.

You then have the layers of the hive containing the hanging racks of sheet wax for the bees to 'draw' out in either direction and fill with honey.

When they have filled each little hole they cap it over with wax to seal it – then and only then is it really ready to take out.

You use a special metal tool (or an old screwdriver if you can't find it) to ease the frame up from where it is invariably also stuck down and then lift it out, gently sweeping any bees hanging around off with a soft brush. I always have a replacement frame to swap in for them to start all over again.

There is a key to this stage, and that is to stay calm. The bees can smell fear and so whilst I wouldn't say I LOVE bees at close quarters, what I do really love is talking myself down to a calm place. This is no place to be in a rush, shout at anyone or be snappy. In fact, it's the one place where you literally have no choice but to behave how I really wish I behaved all the time.

I talk to the boys how I wish I always talked to them. Calmly chatting about what we are going to do next and which frame to take out and where to put it.

You have no choice but to be 100 per cent focused on what you are doing. You cannot use or answer the phone, you cannot deviate or be distracted.

A frame is bizarrely so much heavier than you would expect once it is full of golden honey. One by one, you take the frames out – calmly use the soft brush to slowly sweep the bees off either side – and place into a super frame beside the hive.

Slowly and surely, you swap the frames one by one from this layer and any below, which are called 'supers' – they are slightly shallower than the bottom layer that you don't go in to harvest honey, just to check on the queen.

You continue until you feel you'd had your share of honey and then you put the hive back together and leave with your treasure.

There is a layer beneath all the supers that is called a queen excluder, which is a bit like the grill tray from your oven but with smaller holes. This enables everyone but the one queen to get through and store honey; the queen is slightly larger and she can't fit through, so she stays beneath this layer where it's safe.

Her home is within another layer with frames; this is the bottom layer (called a brood box). This is the honey for the heart of the colony, and where the queen lays her eggs to make more bees and lives in the luxury she deserves.

And does she deserve it!!! A queen will lay up to 2,000 eggs a day in the height of the season and up to one and a half million in her active life.

She collects up to six million sperm all in one to two weeks at the beginning of her adult life, five to six days after emerging from a queen cell. These weeks are filled with non-stop wild flights out where she will mate with twelve to fifteen bees per flight. Once the sperm is collected in those couple of weeks, the rest of the queen's life will be all about making babies as she will store the collected sperm until needed.

So roughly this is how it works with a bee: a non-fertilised egg is a male and a fertilised one is a female (worker bee). The queen will make a male or female baby depending on what the colony needs at the time.

A colony has around 10 per cent (about 400) male bees (drones) and they literally do nothing apart from sitting around eating honey, waiting for an opportunity to go and mate. A male honeybee will fly out and congregate with other drones and hope to be one of the lucky ones to be chosen by a queen to mate with – though it will be the last thing he does as the drone's abdomen is ripped out in the process. If unselected he will return daily. If unsuccessful on these flights, any remaining drones are ejected from the colony when it locks down for winter to preserve as much food as possible for the queen and the worker bees. A drone or male bee cannot survive outside of a colony.

Meanwhile the female worker bees effectively feed the queen and the babies. The social setup of bees is mind-blowingly organised and efficient. Keeping the colony alive is their one single drive and self-sacrifice is just the norm.

When you prize a hive apart and remove the honey, you can't help but feel that you are an intruder to a world of perfect harmony. But it is a respectful relationship and your assistance with how they live by giving them fondant (effectively icing) for them to eat in leaner times and providing them with a ready-made comb to fill with honey hopefully makes it a more balanced relationship than it sometimes feels.

There is something utterly magical though in so many ways about it. It is humans taking a bit of the offcuts from nature whilst ensuring that there is plenty left.

Surely *THAT* is what we should be trying to achieve with all farming. If we could rebalance what we take and leave more behind by only taking what we need rather than what we want – namely consuming less and reusing ideally but if not, only having recyclable materials that are always recycled – things might be looking rosier all round.

Deep down inside I would like to be the person who is able to be so calm and so controlled that I can check my bees suit-free as some people seem to have the confidence to do, but I am not sure I will ever get there – remember the pain/pleasure balance? Well I do!

Bees though are the best pets in the world – of this there is no doubt in my mind. They are the companions, which, when compared with all other pets, are the lowest maintenance and give back bountiful times what you have to put in. Here's how to keep them.

Everything you need to know about beekeeping

There are all sorts of fancy different types of beehive but the boringly normal British National Beehive is by far the most common for a good reason – it's brilliantly straightforward to build and harvest from. You can buy one new or get a second-hand one to start with, and you only need the bare minimum of layers. You can either buy the whole thing assembled and ready to go for about £500 or piece it together here and there for about £100 or sometimes even less.

To have a hive you literally just need enough space for it. However, you do need to consider that the bees need food – ideally lots of varieties of flowers at different times of the year. Bees also need water, so a stream or pond nearby is ideal, and they also would rather not be disturbed too much. So whilst I have met a few urban beekeepers who even keep their beehives on the roof of a block of flats, our farm was pretty perfect.

You do need to know your stuff to get going. Although I was taught the basics by my brother, I also joined the local beekeepers' association and signed up for a six-week beekeeping course on Zoom, which I loved. It was during lockdown, and I would take my glass of wine and leave everyone else in the family to get on with supper and the evening without me whilst I learnt all about bees.

I learnt that . . .

Honey will tend to taste of whatever the bees have been eating. Personally, I'm not a big fan of garlic honey but other than that pretty much anything goes. There is just something about knowing it's your own honey that is really wholesomely fabulous.

I don't think I'd ever really want to gear up our honey production. Perhaps a third hive might be on the cards but I doubt I'd go further than that. You can manipulate how much honey you harvest by keeping a closer eye on the bees and what they are up to, and ensuring that they never swarm (fly away) by nipping out unsuitable queens or bees and even clipping the queen's wings. You can add super layers and harvest at exactly the right time to maximise production.

But for hands-off, chilled beekeeping like mine, I probably take around twenty to twenty-five full frames of honey a year between the two hives I currently have and leave the rest for the bees to enjoy the fruits of their labour.

The lovely owner of a local shop did ask if they could stock it, but I am not sure I am quite ready to sell it despite Laurie being super keen to turn my calming hobby into a money-spinner!

We can't eat the amount of honey we make – my brother spins his frames out more than I do, but then he does have a honey spinner. I have to borrow his honey spinner, but either way we just don't seem to eat as much honey as I thought we would.

Honey has certainly replaced the tiny amount of sugar we used to eat anyway. It has actually made me realise that as a family we eat a massive amount of salad and vegetables – and somewhat weirdly butter – but it is so lovely to have honey on tap and even lovelier to be able to give away as a treasured gift to the people we love. And, if all else fails, honey poured on parsnips or ham when cooking is always a winner!

28

How to be a happy grandparent

One of the driving factors for moving to Somerset was my father and Graham's mother.

When I was young we had a home in the country, and then my mother died and my father remarried. He was very happy living with my stepmother and they, unlike modern parents but quite normal for the day, had a totally separate life from mine. Twenty-five years later my stepmother passed away and a couple of years after that, my father married for the third time to a lovely lady now called Granny Jane who is much-loved in our family.

But my father and Boo, and then Jane, had their own friends, social life, hobbies and entertainments and there was little crossover into mine. This had the massive benefit of leaving me footloose and fancy free to leave home and move to London and make my own life there.

I met Graham, set up home with him, had our own babies and worked out a way of juggling work and childcare with a mixture of babysitters, nannies and friends.

It's not that we didn't see grandparents – we did – but Graham's parents lived in a Hampshire village and mine in a Sussex village and we lived in London. We went and visited and they came to visit when our diaries coincided, but our lives evolved to be independent of each other.

There was never a moment when in 'need' that we'd contact them. So instead, to see them, we'd have to make sure we had a clear day or weekend with all other 'needs' dealt with elsewhere (whether it was childcare or dog- or cat-sitting, etc.).

The result of this in a busy life is that on a day-to-day basis, with more pulls on your time as your children grow, when you have less and less free time for socialising at all – including grandparents – it gets trickier and trickier to 'fit them in' because your children need you more than ever and so does your career to pay for it all.

The trouble is this also comes at the perfect time where, assuming you have roughly thirty-year generations, your parents start to need you too.

And that is when something changes. Your parents stop being parents and become something different – it's not that they are children, but fundamentally you begin to play the parental role in the relationship. Though your parents haven't quite embraced their role of being children, so you are playing the parental role whilst pretending to still play the child role and your parents are pretending to play the parental role whilst actually playing the child role. It is no different from helping your children, except with your children it's all out in the open who is parenting who, but with the generation up it's wrapped up in complicated layers of pretence.

I have a dream – in my utopian dream (largely based on *The Waltons* as previously discussed), three (or even four) generations would live harmoniously in one place entertaining, supporting and enjoying each other's company.

The trouble with this is that it works best from the beginning. There are upsides and downsides to every situation and I would imagine that it's hard to have independent, free-spirited children if you make it really clear you'd really rather they didn't leave home – or indeed when they did you sold up and moved next door. Then there is a danger that they spend the rest of their lives trying to get away from you.

It's hard to find the balance between being the grand-parents that are the 'go-to' for childcare when you go away for the night (to friends or to a wedding or even a little city break together or have to spend the night away with work) and not having them become effectively a full-time nanny supplying free childcare, and they end up not seeing their own friends or having their own interests as they don't have time.

What I do see though is that all the grandparents who made the sacrifice, which is often what is needed in some way, shape or form, to live closer to their grand-children tend to not regret it.

This is often done either by selling their home and pooling resources with their children, or by them moving to a place they are not so familiar with. This new area may not be so ideal on paper but from the experiences of people I have met they are likely to get so, so much more out of it.

If I had to do a straw poll of 'happy grandparents', then those who have sacrificed their living accommodation well before they needed to and focused on the two generations' needs beneath them are just having a better time.

One grandmother I know has a single storey timber annex in the garden and comes and goes on various artistic trips – her capital has been freed up and handed over, with a small amount to live on that doesn't need to be much.

I also have some gorgeous friends who are grandparents and live nearby. They bought the nearest home they could to their grandchildren. It definitely was NOT the house of their dreams, but having a tiny bungalow on the other side of a field to the next two generations enables them to be on tap for childcare, pop over for tea and do the school run several times a week. Plus the grandchildren get to flit between their parents' and grandparents' homes depending on what they want to chat about.

I was lucky enough to be invited to this friend's eightieth birthday lunch and her mind is full of a vast variety of subjects, which she can chat about easily and entertainingly, quite unlike many at her age or even half her age, as she exercises her brain regularly with the comings and goings and conversation of the many generations.

It would be easy to think these choices are straight-forward when you are fortunate, but be very careful indeed of judging the outside of someone else's life from the inside of your own. I know these two lovely families and their stories are not mine to tell, but it is fair to say that they have had more than their fair share of pain and suffering, but they made positive choices at every crossroads they came to and I'm bowled over in admiration of their spirit.

My own mother-in-law bravely moved in lockdown to be less than twenty minutes away from both us and my brother and his wife. She left a village she had been in for decades with dozens of great friends around her to be closer to two of her children (her other lovely son and his family inconveniently don't live in Somerset – though we all live in hope!). She moved when she was, and still is, very able-minded and -bodied but I still don't think it has been that easy. Despite being so close, we don't see her as much as we'd like as somehow life gets in the way of the best of intentions. She is sociable and charming, but making a whole new network of friends is hard even with a family around and doing it on your own in your early eighties takes courage and energy.

So why am I telling you about all these grandparents?

Because somewhere in the move, I thought maybe, just maybe, if we moved to Somerset I might be paving the way to enable this to happen. I think it's harder in a city with less space and anyway I knew that Graham was never going to be settled in London.

You are either an active member of an extended family or you are a visitor. Both are fine but I'm not sure it's possible to switch between the two, and if you don't want to be a visitor you need to put the groundwork in and that can be hard work.

My personal view? Whilst I think the older generation is a wonderful font of years of experience when I am old I would like the younger generation not to feel they owe me anything. The greatest thanks my children can give me, should they want to, is to bring up the next generation with kindness and look after the beautiful planet we live on as best they can.

I do what I do as a parent because I want to and whilst gratitude is a nice added extra, I'm not sure I am entitled to gratitude as my actions are my own choice.

Choice and responsibility are the two things that I have. Choice for my actions but largely choice for how I feel about and respond to the world around me.

We cannot affect large amounts of what happens in life but we can CHOOSE how we feel about it.

We can choose to respond to things in a way that makes our own and other people's lives a bit better – or a bit worse.

I sometimes think if we all focused a bit more on responsibilities rather than rights, we might end up with a happier climate for everyone to live in. My dream is that we all consider our collective responsibilities before we consider our rights to things.

I personally feel a responsibility to the older generation not so much because they have a right to be cared for, which I think they do, but more because I feel a sense of duty to make sure they are cared for.

This isn't a fundamental shift in thinking but it does mean that if everyone considered a tiny bit more what they could give instead of what they can get, then they, as well as everyone else, would be happier.

29

My diagnosis

I started writing this book before I was diagnosed with breast cancer. So whilst I wanted to include it, it is not who or what I intend to be defined by in the future so I thought I'd keep it inside one chapter, which, if you don't want to read, you can just skip.

I would have loved to have perforations in this book so it could be torn out, which is actually a metaphor for how I would like to treat this part of my life when it's all over!

It is a period of my life that is just what it is and, luckily for me, with the diagnosis I had, modern science and the wonderful NHS, it is just a little blip that I have every intention of rubbing out.

My mother died when I was ten. She had what I now know is called a radical mastectomy, which effectively leaves your chest almost concave with no muscle and a rapier scar from under your arm well into your cleavage with white stitch marks to either side. Despite this, somehow, I hadn't realised she had cancer. I was only four when she was diagnosed and my brother was six and it was a different era, but six years later, when she was thirty-nine, her breast cancer had spread to her brain.

She passed away peacefully in my parents' bed a few hours after she fell asleep to me reading her a book (which being a reluctant reader must have meant I knew she didn't feel great).

Looking back, I realise I probably could have worked it out but somehow my mind didn't let me. Day by day you just cope with things and whilst there is a sadness and loss that never leaves you, your life continues and heads down another path.

Forty years later – with a husband and four children, who, despite driving me mad at times, I wouldn't change for the world; a brother and his family, who drive me much less mad but I also wouldn't change for the world; extended family I cherish more than you can imagine; a career in TV; several businesses under my belt and a beautiful home in the countryside – the path I have ended up on is one I wouldn't change for the world.

Here, though, is the nub of it. Even if it meant that my mother would still be around today, I wouldn't change a thing as one thing is for certain: life would DEFINITELY not be how it is today and whilst it conceivably could have been better, that would not be a gamble I would be prepared to take.

I think the loss of my mother when she was thirty-nine gave me rocket fuel in terms of impatience. When your natural role model didn't make it to forty, turning that age myself was a bit of a weird experience, but packing in a lifetime before forty was essential to me.

So when I turned fifty last summer, I thought I was well out of the water. Until I was diagnosed with breast cancer about six months later.

In some ways I had planned it for forty years.

Or perhaps 'planned' is an overstatement but more 'assumed' it. I had routed out various ways of getting checks well before genetics and breast cancer were the norm in conversation.

I did ultrasound checks, mammogram checks – in short, I was probably just a bit more neurotic than most people and planned the fact that I would just remove my breasts if there was the slightest sign of anything.

In fact, when Angelina Jolie was all over the press talking about the BRCA gene mutation, it gave me fuel to test myself genetically – although I hadn't quite managed to do this before I was diagnosed anyway.

I think when I turned forty though, I entered a part of my life I didn't really expect to have. It was weird in lots of ways but an untrodden path and so I perhaps did worry a lot less, as I somehow imagined I must just be a totally different sort of person and therefore had dodged this bullet.

But in the last nine months since then, I have realised

how little I knew, how disproportionate to the actual risk those views were and have found the silver lining in it. Without my mother and people like her having to sacrifice not watching their children grow up, research would not have been done, research that means I *will* see my grandchildren grow up and for that I am so eternally grateful. I will just have to do the parenting and grandparenting for the both of us!

Getting cancer is a rollercoaster ride. You suspect but hope you're being neurotic. You are diagnosed and when they say, 'You have cancer,' what you actually hear is: 'Which coloured coffin would you like?'

Then what came out of my mouth was a reaction based on forty-year-old knowledge of cancer and the forty-year-old treatments that I had only heard my father talking about second hand, often totally out of any context. It took the spectacularly patient breast surgeon and breast care nurse some time to bring me round to listen to a few things through my slightly hysterical reaction to my diagnosis.

Firstly, I had an 80 per cent chance of a 100 per cent cure. That took them several times of saying it for me to actually listen. Then it was two weeks after that that my brother pointed out that didn't also mean a 20 per cent chance of dying tomorrow.

Secondly, my initial suggestion that they cut off both my breasts instantly was possibly not the best course of action, as I definitely needed chemotherapy, due to the type and size of the tumour. If I was to have chemo-therapy first then they could see if it was working, and if not adjust accordingly as chemotherapy is a cocktail of drugs mixed up bespoke each time.

Chemotherapy, whilst pretty heavy-going, will attack the tumour in your breast, but if microscopic bits have floated off around your body and don't show up on your scan, it will zap those too – so it's a bit of an insurance policy. I liked the idea of that.

I would then need a mastectomy, radiotherapy and reconstruction.

I seriously considered for a moment or two how much simpler it would be if I didn't tell anyone at all and just got on with the treatment. After all, there wasn't much point in everyone else worrying about it, and I feared worry about it they would.

If you are lucky enough to have people who love you around you when you are ill, they have their own suffering as they are left just watching and worrying impotently. Worse, they are not expected to struggle with things but instead must be strong and supportive all the time.

But about ten minutes later I realised that was absurd and phoned Graham, told him and then asked him to phone my brother. I then phoned one of my dearest friends and trusted colleague, Angie, who I knew would be full of solutions and dark humour, which is just what I needed and indeed just what she delivered.

When you are diagnosed with breast cancer, it's a rollercoaster ride. But it also meant I just had to lift up the carpet under which I had spent forty-odd years sweeping things I don't really want to deal with.

Underneath there was quite a lot of stuff that was much better left, to be honest, but what there also was, was a load of stuff that wasn't nearly as bad as I thought it was going to be once I faced it head on.

The upsides

It wasn't one of the kids or indeed any of the other kids I am lucky enough to love.

I had a family around me who are funny, kind and supportive.

We have a lovely home and can afford food on the table.

It was 80 per cent curable and, even if it wasn't, as Diccon pointed out, it would be likely that I'd get another ten to fifteen years on the planet with various treatment options, and that would see all the boys grown up. And if I didn't make it to old age, I wouldn't end up grumpy, loopy and a complication for those I loved.

I'd be tested to the ends of the earth and back, so all the undiagnosed tumours that all neurotic people worry about would be found and treated.

I'd get all this treatment paid courtesy of the NHS,

like a massive tax rebate, and could make grateful jibes to friends about how much I was enjoying all their hard-earned cash that had been paid in tax.

I'd get to have no hair and though I didn't have the nerve to do that voluntarily, I had always slightly wondered what it would be like to have a smooth, hair-free head.

Most of my work I could carry on doing, stopping me from going mad by doing nothing. My work also gave me the most amazing ability to hunt down and talk to the top people, and share the information with anyone who cared to listen about the whole process, as I decided to do a documentary on what I was going through. This also might help other people going through the same process. Investigating is what I have done for thirty years about all sorts of subjects and I didn't see cancer as being any different.

I learnt to really appreciate my dear, dear friends – the support I had from family, friends and people I had never met was something I will never forget and will never be able to repay. I will be forever grateful to dozens of thoughtful and kind people, there are so many that made such a massive difference and the constant joyous silliness from soulmates like Angie, Pip and Alex amongst so many others is what got me here today. They will never know how grateful I am for it. There were so many messages of goodwill, each one holding me stable in a rough sea. This overwhelming and extraordinary generosity is what I will never be able to thank people enough for.

The downsides

Your head is cold and losing your hair is a much more emotionally charged thing to happen than I realised.

You also lose your nasal hairs, and so when you get a cold snot just falls out rather than tickling long enough to get a tissue.

You get steroids to counteract the side effects of the chemo but they mean you don't sleep – currently it is 4.42 a.m. and I have been awake since 12.30 a.m.

You get a steroid downer. During my second treatment I got muddled and took them for an extra day – forty-eight hours later I had such an emotional crash that I couldn't even make a phone call. Graham tried all methods of talking to me until a couple of hours later he suggested it might possibly be my meds that weren't quite right as it seemed that the empowered fifty-year-old woman he was married to had turned into an insecure, sobbing wreck.

After he made me several more cups of tea, I realised there was some sanity in what he had said and things didn't seem nearly so bad. The next day I asked the chemo nurses and they confirmed this was entirely normal.

I decided not to drink alcohol during cancer treatment. This I really, really, miss. It wasn't that I was told to cut it out, but a hangover on top of chemo would be quite something to deal with and I am not good at the half-a-glass-once-a-week type of drinking.

I also figured that my liver and kidneys were being asked to do a lot processing of the chemo drugs and I'd give them a helping hand. To be honest, the chemo isn't as bad as some hangovers I have had, so I think I have practised over the years in some ways for the side effects!

You are at a much higher risk of getting really ill, so you need to avoid getting ill at all if possible. This means socialising loses its appeal and anyway you are more tired, so the evenings are a bit of a write-off. I also find no wine takes the sparkle off a good night out.

All the above makes it a bit boring, to be honest, but I am so lucky to have much on my plate, and lovely family and friends to chat to and make me laugh.

There are side-effects that you didn't realise were even possible: terrible indigestion; your mouth burns if you use anything minty apart from children's toothpaste; I got a blocked/infected saliva gland that made my whole face swell up; you puff up; you have a weird taste in your mouth, which is difficult to get rid of, whilst also feeling overwhelmingly thirsty all the time.

I found a new love that is very diluted summer fruits squash, which I have never drunk before and suspect will never drink again, but it's good. Your fingernails hurt to touch anything, like popping out pills from a pill packet. Your toenails throb when you walk across the room or put shoes on. I was lucky as some people's nails all fall out but mine just hurt.

The chemo is delivered via a PICC (peripherally inserted central catheter) line, which they suggested I have fitted. It is like a cannula but it goes into your upper arm and they somehow feed a tiny tube a foot or so long down your vein, ending just above your heart. It stays there for months until all your treatments are finished – it is optional, but it saves needles all the time. They flush the PICC line and redress it every week in the hospital (I was offered that my husband or kids could be shown how to do it but that was definitely one step too far!).

They talk of 'rounds', which for my type of cancer basically means sitting in a chair where they plug you in and drip stuff into you for around an hour or two a round – this is done every three weeks unless you haven't recovered enough when they do a blood test the day before, in which case they put it off for another week or so.

In the first few weeks there are masses of extra appointments of further checks, scans of all your organs and more detailed scans of areas that might be of concern, but luckily all mine were clear.

There are phone calls every three weeks with the

oncologist, who deals with the drugs generally for chemo as well as anything else and its dosage.

Alongside this there are also ultrasounds every two rounds to measure the tumours (I had three) and see if they are shrinking. Though my type of tumours tend not to shrink I discovered; it's more like they are dissolved.

Then you need to consider the surgery and radio-therapy. My chemotherapy was luckily working and so there was some uncertainty as to whether radiotherapy was still necessary.

I discovered that radiotherapy is not without its down-sides either. Firstly, you can only have it once, so if you got a recurrence of the cancer you would have used up your trump card. Secondly, it does affect the tissue and organs nearby to a lesser or greater degree. Thirdly, if you have a mastectomy, the remaining cancer cells have been removed and if they don't find any cancer cells in your lymph glands when they remove a few in surgery and look at them really thoroughly in a laboratory then there aren't any cancerous cells to give radiotherapy to.

I have learnt that a lumpectomy, which they call breast-saving surgery, together with radiotherapy, gives the same outcome as a mastectomy. A lumpectomy is generally done when the tumour is small and is in a fleshy part of the breast so relatively easily removed with surgery.

I also learnt that if you want a reconstruction you can generally have one at the same time as the mastectomy.

There are two ways of doing this: one is by using the fleshy part from the bottom of your stomach (effectively giving you a tummy tuck). They then stretch the rest of your stomach down and make a new tummy button position – a breast surgeon does the cutting out of the cancer and breast tissue and then whilst you are asleep the reconstructive surgeon takes over and does their part. It is expected to be around a seven-hour operation and is not something you bounce back quickly from.

The other skin- and nipple-saving reconstructive option is to cut under your boob, scoop out the contents and stick in an artificial boob – a bit like a shaped beanbag but the stuff inside isn't as bobbly as beans!

You may be offered a reduction at the same time with either of the above reconstructions.

If you have a full mastectomy without a reconstruction at the same time and still want one, they will need to find other skin to make the boob out of and this is generally where the flesh is taken from the bottom of the tummy or from your inner thighs.

In short, you are better off in terms of the end result if you want to reconstruct, saving the skin (or envelope as they call it) in the first place and reconstructing at the same time as you have the mastectomy if that is an option.

Because of my mother, I was tested for BRCA 1 and 2 genes. If you have a mutation in the BRCA1 or BRCA2 gene, you have a high chance of getting another new breast cancer and also of getting ovarian cancer. I was told that should I test positive, then the option of removing the other 'healthy' breast would be something we should discuss but it was unlikely that any surgeon would consider just chopping it off otherwise.

I tested negative for BRCA genes but positive for a less well-known one called PALB2, opening up a whole new can of worms I didn't even know existed.

The fallout of testing positive for PALB2 was that there would be a fifty–fifty chance I could have passed it onto my children, and also that my brother had a fifty–fifty chance of carrying it – and if he did have it then there was a fifty–fifty chance he could have passed it onto his children.

Also, because my father is now quite confused and my mother dead, I would be unable to test them – so needed to go out and down on the family tree to let people know that they could test if they wished to.

The trouble with testing is that you have to be careful to consider exactly why you are testing and most importantly what you are going to do with the information if the outcome is positive.

I dug really deep into this subject and the advantage for me personally was that knowing my risk of getting a new breast cancer was rather higher with PALB2 than if I didn't have it, I was able to have a bilateral mastectomy, i.e. both boobs, thereby reducing the risk of breast cancer to a negligible one as I didn't have any real boobs left.

I decided to do this largely because I was undergoing surgery for one boob, and figured I'd be under the knife and asleep anyway so might as well do them both together and get it over and done with.

I am not totally sure I would have had surgery on my other boob if I hadn't been undergoing surgery anyway. The decision was based on percentages I was given by the consultants. They said as they would be checking it closely the chances were another tumour would be found early. Therefore whilst I'd have to go through all the same treatment all over again I would be as likely to survive as I would be if they removed it as a preventative measure. Knowing there was a fifty–fifty chance I'd get cancer in the other side (up from about fourteen per cent in the rest of the population), I decided to go ahead.

You have to bear in mind though that MOST people get breast cancer from fifty-five to eighty years old, and so the 'risk graph' is weighted heavily towards the older/ my demographic, not the younger one.

PALB2 also gives me a marginal increased risk of ovarian cancer, it is only a small day surgery to remove your ovaries and, as I have had quite enough children and my ovaries are no longer functioning, I am due to have my ovaries removed too.

The complication if my children test positive for PALB2 is not currently relevant. Whilst boys can get breast cancer, a PALB2 diagnosis takes the chances of getting it from infinitesimally unlikely to a bit more than infinitesimally unlikely, so whilst vigilance is key there isn't an urgency – they wouldn't be able to be tested to see if they carried the gene mutation until they were over eighteen anyway.

Then, IF they tested positive and IF they had a daughter, she could choose to be tested at eighteen and IF they were positive, the only change would be for her to be extra vigilant and she would have more regular checks from twenty-five years old, when her risk of breast cancer would be increased.

Again, the greater risk for the non-existent grand-daughters I might one day have would be when they are around fifty years old, when it could be considered wise with current science that, as they would be likely to be post-children, they could consider a preventative mastectomy and perhaps removing their ovaries.

I figured that, considering how far cancer treatment has come in the last forty years and the action for any of this would be decades down the line and so is likely to be very different from now, it was best to not worry about it.

My brother tested and he was not PALB2, and I passed on the information to my aunt and cousins for them to do with as they wished.

This information about PALB2 has informed some preventative decisions I have made, but I would add I think that's probably ONLY because I am the age I am and at the stage I am. It is a deeply individual decision you have to make but one based largely on stats. Personally if I was much younger I would definitely not have undergone the radical preventative extra surgery I have now had. However, I would have been much more insistent that the lump I found, which was given the all clear by a mammogram, was scanned and biopsied several months before it ended up being diagnosed. So the knowledge of my unusual gene and its effects wouldn't really have changed anything – so you could argue what would have been the point in knowing?

There is one big point though. Gene research for cancer is the key. The more that we know about different cancers and why they grow, how they grow and how to kill them, and the more we understand about why those cancers grow in different environments i.e. the genes of the person who is the host to the cancer, the LESS that is needed in terms of treatment.

In fact, what I have learnt is that over the last forty years and looking forward to the next forty years, the holy grail is to minimise treatment ideally to a point where you aren't really affected by it at all.

It's a bit like having a greenhouse full of plants and there is one weed you don't like. If you sprayed toxic poison in the greenhouse, it would kill the weed but also everything else. Just as a dead person doesn't have cancer growing anymore.

The more you understand that particular weed though, and what it lives off and how it thrives, and the more you understand the greenhouse temperature, soil type, etc., the more you can make the environment so hostile for that particular weed that it just can't grow whilst your lettuces and tomatoes flourish.

I approached having breast cancer in not a dissimilar way to how I have approached many things in my life. I decided to make it my personal mission to find out as much as I possibly could about it. I realised that the tiny nibbles of information I knew created an entirely out-of-proportion fear that I had carried for forty years, the more I researched current breast cancer breakthroughs the more interested I became and the more I realised how far things had come since my mother was ill. I think the disabling fear of cancer many people hold is actually often disproportionate to the actual risk with today's modern medical science let alone tomorrow's.

As my son Charlie said – when you think about cancer you only think about the people who have died from it, and when you think about it more, there are MASSES of people we know who have had cancer and are now totally fine, have moved on and are not defined by it at all.

Once you realise how incredible treatment is now, you would be mad not to get to a doctor as soon as you have the tiniest concern as the earlier the diagnosis, the better the outcome.

Even if you are given the all-clear, if the concern is still with you then go back and get a second opinion from elsewhere.

Some thoughts on the National Health Service

I wrote an entire chapter on the NHS that I was counselled to remove but know the following:

I am eternally grateful to the NHS.

To really help the NHS we have to make some radical changes and I believe these need to be agreed cross party so it can be a twenty not four-year plan.

I would encourage everyone to invest in what matters for fifty years' time. The next generation of teachers, doctors, nurses, artists and scientists are crucial, and I would question the wisdom of them having to run up huge debts to train for these roles in particular.

All my other opinions I will leave for the time being!

30

Ukuleles, Pam Ayres and our very own Glastonbury

With all that has been going on in my life in the last year, you would have thought I'd prioritise slowing down, but instead I've found myself asking one question: so what next?

I made what I considered to be a funny comment to a young crew member a couple of years ago and realised from the slight rolling of their eyes that I am definitely getting old. I decided to make 'age appropriate' comments in future.

Ageing is not a bad thing. I like wrinkles as they tell the story of your life. Young faces are so beautiful and clear but have no wisdom laid on them – that is all to come. I do wear make-up though, and will continue to dye my hair. I think working 'with' nature is my plan, not against it – although I make no judgements of anyone who does, whatever way they wish.

I can't imagine 'retiring' – I think I'd be too bored

- and I think it's a good idea to have a new career every ten years or so anyway to stop you getting complacent.

Who knows what life will bring next for a middle-aged woman, one who hasn't ever really enjoyed following any rules. Life now has different opportunities, exciting ones that wouldn't have been there thirty years ago.

Music and following the progress of Graham and the boys' band, The Entitled Sons, is definitely one of those opportunities. Every day a new success seems to come: a brilliant song written and released, being asked to play at a new gig, one of their songs being played on the radio or filming a music video. I know I'm only a mascot but that doesn't stop me enjoying every second of it with them. When my brother and I were young, my mother patiently pushed us both to learn the piano. My only memory of my parents playing instruments is my father, who played the clarinet at school in a band and still had it when we were children. Generally late at night he would get it out and do what can only be called jamming.

He wasn't a 'cool' dad who liked pop music, but he did like jazz and he did like lots of other choral and symphonic music. He also played the piano but he'd never learnt, he just somehow had taught himself to sort of ride the jazz blues chords whilst making a lot of noise, but to me it sounded gritty and fun. My mother I don't think played the piano, but she was sent away to boarding school at four years old so I am not sure she got the chance. Her mother, a highly driven and a successful working woman who worked in the fashion industry in London, was definitely not the sort of mother who sat next to her daughter patiently teaching her to tinkle on the ivories!

In fact, one of the few tales I know of my mother's childhood was how my grandmother had a baby grand Steinway piano, which, heartbreakingly, she paid someone to take away (Steinways are arguably the best and most expensive pianos costing £50,000-plus in today's money). So growing up we didn't have a Steinway. We had an old piano someone was getting rid of but nevertheless our mother would sit next to us and cajole us into practising.

There were some local music competitions at the time. I am not sure if it was the piano teacher or my mother who entered us but much of my first ten years on the planet was based around these competitions. You'd stand up one by one in a village hall somewhere and perform to a table of three judges, who would find winners for each category and award medals and rosettes to those who they considered best. We were entered in masses of these categories. First it was a piano, and then I started playing the flute and Diccon the trumpet.

We also did the poetry reading category where I learnt the joys of Pam Ayres and classics such as 'Ozymandias'. We entered the singing competition, where one of my most excruciating performances was singing

'Where Is Love?' from *Oliver!* and not remembering any of the words. Apart from this episode, Diccon and I generally won. In fact, I think the other parents found us quite annoying because of this (or maybe we were quite annoying anyway but also won!).

We didn't win because we were the best as, let's be honest, banging out some tedious Grade 1 piano piece is hardly a tell-tale sign of the next Beethoven. We won because of the hours and hours of dedication our mother put into sitting and encouraging us to practise and practise until it was right.

I hadn't really thought about music in my childhood in this way really until writing this book. I think I always assumed that my mother knew she was dying and was trying to pack all her parenting into the short time she had with her children.

I think you could call it pushy parenting, but actually it's a bit more complex than that. Either way, my perception of how she parented us has certainly set the bar at that level for me to not disappoint myself with my own children.

And her dying when I was only ten meant that the fallout and downsides of her what now might be called tiger or helicopter parenting is unknown.

So my children at three or four years old were learning the piano. I sat and cajoled and bribed them to learn. They did just as we did as if you put that much time and effort into something, then it tends to pay off.

Graham didn't learn any instruments as a child and

didn't get tiger-parented into music, but did sing in a band briefly at school although that all dissipated before it ever really took off – despite him singing at gigs at the Astoria and Hippodrome in London (which he reminds the children of on a regular basis and is now a bit of a standing joke between them).

So it wasn't until the boys' utterly brilliant piano teacher in London, Nicole, suggested that Raffey might be better learning a different instrument – as she didn't feel he was going to make progress on the piano as he struggled to hold attention – that we had a look at what we were doing.

Graham got Raffey a guitar – and himself one for good measure – we found a guitar teacher, and Raffey (and Graham) were off.

Before long they were both playing well.

So that was how it started and the playing went on.

Billy was flying at school playing the piano and had taken up the saxophone, inspired by a teacher he liked, and was now playing with various school bands and even went and busked on the local market street with a couple of friends one Saturday (they were all bowled over by their charity proceeds and I didn't like to burst the bubble and point out that basically all our friends had come and watched!!).

Billy and Charlie were both in the school choir (probably made cool by the fact that their older two cousins, Theo and Orlando, were at Westminster Abbey Choir

School and sang at William and Kate's royal wedding!).

Then one day their music teacher asked them to audition to be in a production of *Oliver!* he was the musical director of in the East End of London.

Charlie, blond and, if I'm honest, designed for the part, was asked to play Oliver and Billy was asked to play Charlie Bates (though he will be eternally furious that he wasn't asked to play the Artful Dodger!).

They were both brilliant, and I think this is when Charlie accepted that it probably is his voice that is his first instrument. By some extraordinary luck, a leading acting agent happened to see them one night and asked to represent them both – so there was a flurry of auditions over the next few months and some very enjoyable times spent as a chaperone on the set of *Doc Martin*.

Meanwhile back at home everyone was happily jamming away – Raffey had a natural flair for the guitar and had overtaken Graham, who had moved onto the bass, Billy was on the keyboard and now Charlie was singing.

But to play the odd cover they needed drums, so along came a drum kit from eBay one day. Then they needed someone to play the drums so the obvious thing to do was to get their baby brother to play them.

Laurie was still at junior school aged six, but Raffey, Charlie and Billy were now regulars at all school performances, often performing something together, which they really enjoyed but not half as much as I did!

Music was pretty much everywhere – we went on holiday to Italy once with Diccon, Caroline, Graham's brother Edward and his wife, Annika, and all our children, and we took ukuleles, which are a fine instrument and quite easy to learn as well as travel with.

I think the guy who came and fixed the swimming pool thought we were all mad but we enjoyed singing sea shanties and Irish ballads day and night. This has always been our world, and as the boys grew up they were lucky enough to be inspired by their older cousins' love of music ahead of them, especially the very talented Theo who has released some properly great songs.

And that's roughly how it carried on until we moved to Somerset. We left lovely Nicole and the wonderful Mr Smith behind. That was one of the worst bits of moving.

Sadly I suspect Grade 8 piano will not happen without Nicole, but she got our children to a place where music was already in their bones.

Then I had some luck. I met someone working in a local museum when I visited to while the time away before collecting the children from school. She told me about the museum but also that her boyfriend played the guitar and I asked if he might be prepared to come and teach Raffey.

Five years later, Sydney, as well as his then girlfriend

and now wife Olivia, are wonderful close friends.

It was lockdown where everything changed, particularly for music, as everyone was here – all the time. When he was allowed, Sydney would come and teach Raffey, though at times from outside in the garden through the window. But then Graham would ask Sydney for some tips on learning the bass guitar.

So with them all there, they would all jam together. Actually, it was pretty good. When people were finally allowed to come over again they would be ushered in to listen to 'the band' playing 'Johnny B. Goode' or similar.

They decided to find a name and do a photo shoot, which gave me a role briefly. They settled on naming themselves The Entitled Sons, largely to get in there first before other people called them that. At their first gig they played three of their own songs.

Shortly before this, the boys' eldest cousin, Theo Beeny (check out his music on good old Spotify – always space for a bit of proud auntie nepotism!), who had written a few really fantastic songs in lockdown after coming home from music college in Edinburgh, told them how to release a song on Spotify. They followed his instructions and astonishingly their song 'Break' flew up the iTunes charts.

It was so, so exciting as hour by hour up it went until it actually got to Number 1 in the rock category and Number 31 in the overall hits that week.

And that was where the band really started and they

were approached to play various gigs. So now, a year and fifteen gigs later, two of which were on the main stage at CarFest North and CarFest South with audiences of 30,000 people, they applied for a competition to play at Glastonbury – and won.

So the six of them, four teenagers and their dad, along with Sydney, are heading to Glasto (with me hotly in tow as their chief make-up artist/photographer).

Sydney has actually played there before but for our family the first time we go to Glastonbury will be when they play there – ironic as two years before they had been joking when they said on the school run they didn't think they'd go to Glastonbury until they played there!!?? It is a mixture of excitement and anticipation at home now.

Billy has finished school and deferred his place to study music at Goldsmiths university in London for a year so he can record all the songs that they have been working on.

So this summer we all go to Glastonbury, which is only spurring me on to have the festival I have always dreamt of and what might have been the final sweetener for buying a farm. This year we plan it, and next year I hope to have a carnival celebrating all things that are sustainable, surrounded by music.

Largely probably because I am so excited by the next generation for whom new clothes are a sign of a bit of a failure. In one generation they have managed to rebrand

and celebrate the jumble sales of my youth, and now wear their own brands by finding pieces of clothing no longer wanted and sometimes drastically and sometimes slightly changing them to mean they are useful again.

These young artists who wear their art pieces would be celebrated, along with all the other positive things that are happening when it comes to considering the world about us.

Between that and new, exciting bands (obviously including my nephew, children and husband!), I am hoping we will have a festival that will be a positive and fun way to celebrate all that is so fabulous about individuality, the arts and saving the planet bit by bit.

It's a big thing to organise but I have every hope we can make it work. There aren't many things in my life that I have really wanted to do that I haven't eventually just got on with.

So, as you can see, life goes on here, it never slows down but I wouldn't want it to, and no day is ever the same. Whether it's beekeeping or organising a music festival or even having a film studio – watch this space! – I find it very hard to stand still. I do think I'm getting better at slowing down, but it's a skill I'm certainly still honing.

31

Slowing down and learning how to just 'be'

In the countryside I am in wonderment of the changes that happen every day. I have discovered that even when it's bitterly cold in the winter, those days are beautiful too. Outside the window, nature seems so brutally un-inhabitable in those cold days and yet the wildlife still hardily pushes on through.

I worry about the buds that come through too early in the year on the trees; I watch, tinged with sadness, at the voles the cats bring in and then reflect on the fact that if they can catch them that easily then so can the barn owl that has taken up home in our owl box and I'm glad about that.

It feels like our family has just got bigger, and now instead of the rather annoying caged hamsters and guinea pigs the children had in London, we are surrounded by pets of all shapes and sizes to enjoy as they run and fly free.

It's not that I didn't notice the seasons in London, it's just that I only noticed them very loosely.

There was summer when you could sit on the common with a picnic or outside a restaurant and the rest of the year when you couldn't. That felt like the whole year.

These outside and inside seasons were broken up with a few fun holidays and 'event' days such as Halloween, Bonfire Night, Christmas and New Year's Eve, then a tedious lump of time in January when people are broke/ teetotal/trying to get fit or thin before Easter.

But none of it really related to the seasons. And none of it made me feel grounded in the sense that being here in Somerset does. There is something about being in the country, watching the seasons so closely, that just slows things down.

Slowing down is something I've never been very good at and, with this in mind, my new year's resolution this year was to take up pottering. Pottering, namely doing something relatively pointless, just for the sake of it.

My personal pottering rules can't include planting vegetable seeds but can include planting flower seeds – but only if they definitely won't be back next year. It can include doing jigsaw puzzles, the crossword and reading a random variety of history books simply 'because'.

It can also include sorting out pencil drawers or re-ordering my sock drawer. In short, pottering is what in my before-new-year life was called 'wasting time'.

You see, I have learnt that there is something really and truly glorious about just 'being'. And that holy grail is my planned next achievement.

Allowing myself time to 'be' is something I have always struggled with, more so as I get older. For some reason I have always had a self-inflicted sense of guilt about time passing because 'I just want to' do something.

This started as a fairly reasonable and pragmatic view but the more I ended up taking on, the more I allowed it to grow into a horrible monster.

Well now, being here, watching the world patiently pass by outside, I've decided that monster needs to be hunted down and tackled straight on.

I have a lovely friend called Pip who, whilst being brilliantly talented at many other things, generously spends time with me on my 'pottering' sessions. In fact, she is most excellent at suggesting and arranging some brilliant pottering. Despite being busy with a couple of jobs her delightful way of being, endless creativity and WhatsApp banter is a highlight of many days, particularly over the last year.

We recently walked up Glastonbury Tor to have a cup of tea. Not content with a Thermos mug of tea, she somewhat brilliantly brought a thermos of water, a teapot, teabags, a container of milk, two cups WITH saucers and a carefully sliced Mars bar in a small Tupperware that once contained flakes of sea salt.

Since then, 'tea in random bits of Somerset' is a fabulous new addition to my 'pottering diaries' – though not as regular as I would like, seeing how good it is for my mental health!

Another joyful new frippery is, surprisingly, loo rolls. I have been saving loo roll insides for months now and recently spent a delightful afternoon with my son Charlie carefully filling them with seed compost and popping a variety of flower seeds in them.

Then there are the birds. My brother has managed to get an incredible array of birds to feed from different bird feeders outside his kitchen door. We have all been awestruck by this Attenborough-like show by my bird whisperer of a brother, watching a sensational array of tiny garden birds enjoying his snacks whilst we sip our morning tea.

So, for my birthday, I asked Graham for a bird feeder to attach to the fence outside our kitchen and I'm delighted to report it worked! We had a beautiful blue tit who arrived to enjoy our easy snacks.

Sadly though, food chains work as food chains do and I must confess the feeder became too tempting for one of our cats who about thirty minutes later appeared in the kitchen with what had until recently been an alive blue tit in her mouth.

Clearly the 'drive through' for the blue tit just ended up a 'drive through' for the cats.

Reluctantly I removed the bird feeder – our cats will have to work a little harder and go and catch rats in the barn if they really want live food!

But then a rather lovely finch started sitting on the windowsill on the first floor outside my bedroom window where nothing but a flying cat could disturb anything. For a week it sat there and so I went and collected the bird feeder and with great excitement attached it to the outside of my bedroom window.

The next morning, I sat up in bed with my cup of tea, eagerly awaiting his visit to eat my tasty snack.

He didn't appear and sadly has never returned. I have decided feeding birds is just not my best skill, even though I live in hope as there is nothing I would like more than to have an excuse to make fat balls from leftovers in the kitchen (a very enjoyable thing to do by the way).

All these things have been such lovely bonuses of moving to Somerset.

So what have I learnt from all of this?

I have learnt so much.

I learnt that the children don't care much about sleeping on shared mattresses on the floor or having the order I think matters.

I learnt that all our security is having each other, not about what is around us.

I learnt I was luckier than I ever realised because you can make fun in any situation if you want to enough.

I already thought I was pretty fortunate in the first place but I learnt that, trite as it might sound, home really is where the people you love are.

I learnt that a new adventure only starts when you take a risk – as terrifying as that may be, your bravery will be rewarded tenfold.

Lastly, I have learnt that Graham was right, which is very annoying.

He's right because, with patience and care and time, you can change things. You can build something beautiful. Four years down the line a house has been built and trees and hedgerows are starting to grow. There are now so many different birds that I have to actually look them up to know what they are called.

We find flowers and plants popping up that weren't planted, and thousands of bulbs we have planted come back year after year. There is beauty in the wild nature of the untended garden and beauty in just watching things do what they want to do.

What Graham is more right about though than I had ever appreciated is that slowing down and letting things take a bit more time is actually not as boring as I had thought.

In fact, in many ways, watching the seasons has made me think that now is the time to enjoy what we have.

I feel less guilt than I ever did before. I am coming to the conclusion that you don't HAVE to fill every waking hour with an achievement to not be a failure.

The green I watch out of the window is never a constant – it morphs and moves in its own rhythm and the fact that I can only scratch around the edges of it, because nature has such a strong will of its own, is good for me.

There is pleasure in just 'being' – I haven't quite arrived in the peaceful place I know nature breathes into your veins, but what I have done is allow nature in to start its work on me – and that is definitely a good start.

Epilogue

Now when things don't seem so sunny, which recently they haven't, I have to remind myself: you generally get what you expect. That goes for relationships, experiences, responses, building houses and everything else. In fact, preparing for the worst is a self-fulfilling prophecy and if it isn't, it's even more depressing that you have spent all that time preparing for something horrible that doesn't happen anyway.

It is 100 per cent the most pointless and destructive thing you can do. I personally have to remind myself a lot of this fact, especially with the children where it is only too easy to get into a rut when they behave in a way that you don't like; so you expect them to behave that way and so they do behave that way – and you have spectacularly proved yourself right. The tricky thing is that there is no room in this scenario for children to not behave that way.

Whilst it is exhausting and frustrating, remaining

optimistic is the only possible way that positive things might happen – for never has a truer word been said than 'positive things happen to positive people'. I cannot tell you how often I have just decided there will be a parking space right outside where I want to be – and when I get there, there is one.

I would be lying if I said moving to the country has been easy at all times. It hasn't. It was a massive financial, emotional and practical game of roulette, ending with a dose of breast cancer just as things finally felt like they were all falling into place.

But then, this Christmas, we all gathered together in our beautiful new dining room. We dressed up in black tie, lit candles and celebrated how lucky we all are to have each other, and how lucky Graham and I are to be able to create the home for this delicious family of ingredients to meet and enjoy each other's company.

We have so many magical memories of Christmas at Rise Hall that I was determined to create new magical memories when we moved to Somerset. The start of Christmas at Rise Hall was always when the Christmas tree arrived, a gift from our fabulous neighbours Hugh and Booey. That memory got me thinking: couldn't we have a similar tradition in Somerset? So within weeks of moving, we planted fifty Christmas trees, dotted around the farm. The second year we planted another fifty. Now we are down to planting twenty and next year it will be ten. Soon we will end up only planting five or six a year, but my hope is that in ten or fifteen years' time, we will go with our own farm tractor and trailer and gather our own tree.

Hopefully we will also be able to deliver to some young families the other trees we have grown, to pass on the joy we were lucky enough to have from our lovely neighbours at Rise Hall when we first moved in. I've always loved Christmas – the bigger, the louder, the messier, the more chaotic the better. And tacky.

Unfortunately, Graham is a bit of a taste snob. It's not that I don't like the calm of good taste, but I think Christmas in particular is a great time to throw it all in the air and have more of an eye on fun than sophistication. As a result, we have had many Christmases where the children and I have decorated the tree and long after we are in bed, Graham has tiptoed down to 'fix the tree' as he calls it.

I am a big fan of the dried orange decoration but I am also absurdly sentimental, so the paper chain is a yes from me – but not from Graham. The plastic decoration that one of the children found in a junk shop is a yes from me but not from Graham.

Fortunately, over the years we have grown to find the lack of agreement endearing, unlike how I unload the cutlery from the dishwasher into the drawer, which will be cited in our divorce papers if we ever get there as I am a 'I'm in a hurry; tip it in and sort it later' person and he is a 'NEVER EVER EVER do that' person.

I have a saying, which is 'ghastly good taste'. I always think you have to be super careful that you don't slip into this, and keep half an eye on being a little bit different and allowing the inner child to pop out at times. Graham reckons I would love the house to be lit up so you could see it from space. That is honestly quite true – but he's lucky as whilst I am totally full of admiration of the effort involved and I'm utterly wowed by the best Christmas lights on houses, I am too lazy to actually put that amount of effort into something that has to be taken down a few weeks later. But thank goodness for those who do!!!

We are lucky in our family as Santa visits everyone. It does mean that there is sometimes a bit of a logjam after supper and before bed with various Santas running around the house eating half a carrot and looking for satsumas, but it also means there is a massive amount of talk about Santa. Everyone's stockings are really very much more important than any present under the tree. It is a tradition that I believe all my children and my brother's children will keep up and there is never anyone who misses Father Christmas's touch.

When the children were aged between three to nine years old, we even got a cousin who was staying to dress up in a Santa outfit and run through the trees outside for the children to catch a glimpse of. We had it all planned out totally brilliantly, even giving him a change of clothes to quickly stick on before re-joining us.

Guttingly, the children noticed he was missing so I don't think it worked. I pointed out though they had a binary choice: they could believe and Santa would visit or they could not believe and he wouldn't.

Now, aged thirteen to eighteen, my children all believe. If you asked my brother's kids, aged sixteen to twenty-five, they also all believe as indeed so do I, Graham, Diccon and Caroline.

It is the nonsense of Christmas and the fact it comes only once a year that I love so much. When I was a child, we got the *Radio Times* and I'd highlight what we wanted to watch. It's amazing how many times you can watch a James Bond film or *The King and I* year after year without getting bored.

Of course, the world of streaming has knocked that on the head but still it's a time when as an extended family we are together for an extended period of time.

I had two types of childhood Christmases: the ones with my mother and the ones with my first stepmother, and they couldn't have been more poles apart. Whilst I loved the ones with my mother – I think I loved the ones with my stepmother even more.

My mother's Christmases were quiet and generally just the four of us. They were controlled and organised and lovely. We would carefully take it in turns to open a present each at specific times with specific rules around said opening.

My mother would ensure we all carefully slit the

Sellotape open and the paper would then be folded and later down the line it would be guillotined back into shape and even ironed flat to fit back in the wrapping paper box.

My stepmother's Christmases were full of armies of stepfamily and I don't know what happened to the wrapping paper, but newspapers were rolled up to play games such as 'Are you there, Moriarty?', which involved two people lying blindfolded and face to face on their stomachs, one hand holding the other person's, whilst the other hand held a rolled up newspaper. One then asked the other person: 'Are you there, Moriarty?' and the other person would answer 'yes' and try and move to avoid the questioner from landing a newspaper hit to the head.

There were endless other games such as sardines and word association games that were played.

We still get together as an extended family and we still play games. There is generally a game of Risk going on somewhere – often late into the night. Risk is a game that can make or break friendships – a little like Monopoly, which will also be embedded in a corner somewhere.

As everyone has grown up, the evenings roll on through the night with various invented word games around the table that seem to end with way too many rude words and a few people laughing so much they fall off their chairs.

Our personal 'take' on charades involves someone

leaving the room and coming back and guessing what everyone is doing in some shape or form. This also invariably ends up with an awful lot of laughter.

But in the end, I don't think it's the games that make Christmas so magical or the fish pie that somewhere along the line morphed into a beef Wellington, provided for Christmas Eve by whoever isn't hosting Christmas Day. I think it's the combination of everything and the sheer belief that everyone has before turning up that there is no possibility we won't have a totally brilliant time.

And so this Christmas wine flowed, chocolate was eaten, the turkey was overcooked, potatoes under, gravy cold but we had done it – the best of Rise Hall was now in our new home in Somerset.

So do I regret any of this? No. Would I do it again? Most definitely yes. Would I do it the same? Even that I would say yes to – for what I have learnt about myself and gained along the way I feel sure will be the compost I need for the next half of my life to be more interesting, more fulfilling and even better than the first half.

Acknowledgements

I would like to thank all those involved in creating *The Simple Life* at Orion Books. My particular thanks go to: the fabulous Lisa Carter who I couldn't have written this without, my agents Carina Rizvi and Rowan Lawton at The Soho Agency, Angie Robinson who makes all the wheels turn around, Lionel Horler for bee wisdom, and Marc Tischkowitz and all the other amazing specialists who helped me learn so much about cancer and the brilliant cancer treatments of the future. And, of course, I also want to thank my long-suffering husband, Graham; my children, Billy, Charlie, Raffey and Laurie; and my brother, Diccon, and family for their support.

Credits

Seven Dials would like to thank everyone at Orion who worked on the publication of *The Simple Life*.

Agent
Rowan Lawton

Editor
George Brooker

Copy-editor
Clare Wallis

Proofreader
Laetitia Grant

Editorial Management
Susie Bertinshaw
Tierney Witty

Jane Hughes
Charlie Panayiotou
Lucy Bilton
Claire Boyle

Audio
Paul Stark
Jake Alderson
Georgina Cutler

Contracts
Dan Herron
Ellie Bowker
Alyx Hurst

Design
Nick Shah
Jessica Hart
Joanna Ridley
Helen Ewing

Picture Research
Nat Dawkins

Finance
Nick Gibson
Jasdip Nandra
Sue Baker
Tom Costello

Inventory
Jo Jacobs
Dan Stevens

Production
Katie Horrocks

Marketing
Katie Moss

Publicity
Virginia Woolstencroft

Sales
Jen Wilson
Victoria Laws
Esther Waters
Tolu Ayo-Ajala
Group Sales teams across Digital, Field, International and Non-Trade

Operations
Group Sales Operations team

Rights
Rebecca Folland
Tara Hiatt
Ben Fowler
Alice Cottrell
Ruth Blakemore
Ayesha Kinley
Marie Henckel